D1240570

Cover image: Shutterstock

Cover design: Raphael Albinati

Copyright © 2017, by Rivka Levy. All rights reserved.

 Published by Matronita Press

Canada House, Morasha, Jerusalem, Israel

To contact Matronita Press directly, email our Customer Care Department at: **www.matronitapress.com**

Levy, Rivka
        The Secret-Diary of a Jewish Housewife: VOLUME 1: THE MOVE TO THE GOLDEN CITY / Rivka Levy – First edition

ISBN: 978-965-7739-13-6 Trade Paperback

ISBN: eBook

FIRST EDITION

Printed in the USA

For R, M and T, who know all my secrets.

Contents

Introduction

The Secret Diary of a Jewish Housewife contains my secret musings on one of the craziest years of my life.

I wrote it for all the women out there who are also sometimes sick of all the meals we have to make; or exhausted by all the love and empathy we have to provide for our husbands, kids and friends. Read this and be reassured that you aren't the only woman worrying about piling on the pounds, or panicking about whether you're actually even getting *somewhere* in life; (and when that last one hits, only chocolate can really heal the pain.)

This diary starts in January 2015, a few months after me and my family moved to the golden city of Jerusalem and opened up a tourist attraction called 'The Meaning of Life' in the Old City's Jewish Quarter.

Dear reader, the whole thing was a complete nightmare from start to finish!

We arrived in Jerusalem just in time to experience a huge wave of Arab riots, which quickly turned into another of Israel's mini-wars a few days' later, when Operation Protective Edge began to try to stop the hundreds of missiles being fired into Israel from terrorists in the Gaza Strip.

Within a couple of days' of the unrest starting, Jerusalem went from being considered one of the most dangerous places in the country (because of the riots) to one of the safest again (because very few rockets were reaching this far...) But our tourist attraction still died a slow, lingering death.

Four months after we opened the doors, we'd still only managed to sell just seven tickets, and our business was officially a bust. So in November 2014, my husband and I finally pulled the plug on that part of our Jerusalem dream, and 'The Meaning of Life' closed down.

Now, came the really hard part: we had to dig deep, and try to figure out what the meaning of *our* life was going to continue to be, now that we'd lost our business, our savings, and our reassurance that things would somehow always work out OK.

(Let me spoil the cliff-hanger ending here by telling you it DID all work out fine, kind of, in the end...)

This diary is a chronicle of one of the craziest years of my life, a testament to the power of prayer, and a glimpse inside the world of a Jewish housewife who was trying (and usually failing...) to stay sane in a mad world.

The identity crisis

For the last nine and a half years, I've been trying my hardest to be an ISRAELI. I've been hampered in my quest to be an ISRAELI by a couple of major drawbacks: it took me three years before I even had a chance of understanding what my kids' teachers were telling me at the PTA (Even now, I mostly just smile and nod...)

And secondly (and this one I've only just realised) - I'm actually *not* an Israeli.

How can I be? My formative years were spent in London and Canada, and until I was 16 we weren't doing anything very 'Jewish' at home. I went to a non-Jewish school, and I obsessed over all the things my non-Jewish friends obsessed over: George Michael, clothes and Back to the Future.

It's not very spiritual, is it? It's not very Jewish. It's not very ISRAELI.

And for the first twenty years of my life, that's what I had hardwired into to my soul: British non-Jewish culture, with all its sarcastic humour, beer and obsession with pies.

I'd taken a lot of the more obvious rough edges off in London, before I made aliyah. We were keeping kosher, keeping Shabbat, learning Torah, hanging out with Jews.

So in my head, I thought I'd step off the plane at Ben Gurion, pick up Hebrew in two weeks, and then have a bunch of cool sabra friends called Ilanit and Roni to hang out with.

But that's not exactly what happened.

We landed in a very 'Anglo' neighbourhood, and quickly outgrew it. I wanted real Israel; I didn't move to Israel just for my kids to feel like expat Brits. So we moved to an ISRAELI settlement across the Green Line, and I tried my darndest to fit in.

Three years' later, my kids spoke Hebrew really nicely, and their friends were all Israeli, which I thought was so cool, until they started beating my children up on the way to school.

I don't know how a real ISRAELI would have reacted, but I reacted by getting the heck out of there, and moving to a place that was a bit more *civilised* (read: socially repressed) and Anglo.

For the first year, it was heaven. Then all the things that I don't like very much about Anglo culture resurfaced, like the competition to be seen as a 'success'; and the clique-yness; and the obsession with big houses and nice holidays.

This was in my super-duper-trying-to-be-frum-like-people-in-Meah-Shearim period, when I felt bad about doing anything more gashmius than buying a chicken leg for Shabbos.

A whole bunch of things happened over the next three years, and to cut a long story short, we ended up in Jerusalem, very close to Meah Shearim, six short (but very long...) months ago.

Moving to Jerusalem sparked off a whole big identity crisis for me. I realised that I actually didn't want to be chareidi; I realised that I actually didn't want to be poor; I realised that making a good kugel was just not spiritually satisfying, however hard I tried.

And the last thing I realised, in the middle of the Shlomo Katz Chanuka concert I went to last week, is that I actually don't want to be ISRAELI anymore. It's not that any of these things are intrinsically bad, God forbid. They're just not *me*.

After that particular penny dropped, I paid my first visit to the Jerusalem Gap Store for about three years, and I picked up a new coat with fake fur on the hood. It looks so 'Anglo-in-Israel' - and I love it.

I don't know what all this means. What I can tell you is that as I'm reclaiming all these parts of myself that I've been embarrassed or ashamed of, I'm feeling so much happier and settled and healthy.

No more beating myself up for liking beans on toast. No more disdaining myself for actually really liking that nice grey jumper in Zara. No more feeling like a worm, because I'm enjoying listening to music in English for a change (by the Maccabeats...)

I know it was all well-meaning, and spiritually-striving of me to try to be a holy Meah Shearim-type balabusta, but the big drawback was that it's not *me*. I nearly killed myself trying to fit into those boxes, but God has been showing me time and again that I have a different way of trying to build the world, and to get closer to Him, and it entails going through Gap on the way to the Kotel.

What can I do? I know God wants me to serve Him happily, as me. And now that I've got my fake fur trim coat I feel I've taken a giant step towards giving Him what He really wants from me: to be me, even with all my imperfections.

The secret of shemitta year

Sometimes, we experience a time of such prolonged, intense darkness in our lives, that it's called 'The secret of shemitta year'. Before Big Agro came on the scene, keeping shemitta meant letting the land lie fallow for a year, which could mean you'd have no food to eat for a whole 12 months.

Food = parnassa = sustenance = livelihood = the means, the wherewithal to stay alive, to live.

In our times, this sort of potential destitution and economic vulnerability can still happen, but with a modern twist: the bank can foreclose on your house; your job (or business) can disappear overnight; everything you try to do can fail, often inexplicably. After this has carried on for a while, you hit rock bottom, and you start to wonder how you are ever going to make ends meet enough to continue to live, to be.

All your financial security, all your assets, all your confidence in your ability to make a living, evaporates. It's a massive test.

Our rabbis explain that the only way you can pass these sorts of test in one piece is to work really hard on your emuna, and in particular, on your emuna that *Ein Od Milvado* - God is really all there is.

If you can hang on to your faith in the middle of this test - and believe me, it's really not easy - then, our rabbis tells us, you'll see that God Himself is sustaining you, and that He always was, even when you thought it was your great degree, or your amazing real estate acumen, or your fantastic job that was doing it all.

If you can hang on - and again that can be a very big 'if' - then you'll achieve a massive *tikkun*, or soul correction, that will fix a whole bunch of very deep, hard-to-reach things in your soul.

And these tests don't last forever.

When I first read these teachings of our rabbis about the secret of the shemitta year, I almost cried from relief. You see, everything my husband and I have tried for the last two years financially, professionally, socially, religiously - you name it - flopped so badly it went past 'embarrassing' a long time ago.

It got so bad at one point that I started watching the local bag ladies to pick up tips for when I'd have to pack up and move again - to the nearest dumpster.

Until a month ago, I truly couldn't see how we were ever going to turn things around, or how we were going to be able to 'live' in any sense of the word, once the money we got from selling our house ran out.

Then I went to Uman.

I learnt a lot of lessons there, I got a lot of breakthroughs, and one of the biggest presents I came home with was hope, and the feeling that maybe, just maybe, we will be successful again, we will earn money again, we will own a home again, it will be good again.

I know shemitta year is only two months' old for most people (if it's even on their radar), but I feel my own personal shemitta ended in Uman last month. And now, I'm waiting for the good times to roll again, whenever God's ready to send them down.

Words to live by – A woman's sense of purpose

The other day, I was thinking about what my purpose in life, as a Jewish woman, really is. Is it really to help my husband pay our mortgage, and to try and fit my parenting and spiritual growth in around my full-time office job? Or is there something deeper going on here?

After some pondering, and some checking through Jewish sources, it jumped out at me loud and clear that I'm not going to achieve any lasting sense of purpose by trying to be a co-py-cat man.

A man's spiritual role in the world is very different from a woman's spiritual role. So much of our suffering and difficulties stem from the fact that people just don't know this stuff anymore, and have bought into the secular viewpoint that the whole purpose of life for everyone is just to make as much money as possible.

But that's not the Jewish way. So what is? What can really give us Jewish women a lasting sense of purpose, if it's not all the college degrees we have hanging on our walls, and all the money we're making with our big, fat careers?

Each person can decide that for themselves. But in the meantime, I put together the following 'words to live by', based on our Jewish sources, to help you (and me...) along the path to clarity.

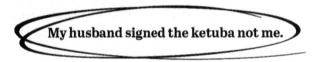

My husband signed the ketuba not me.

The Arizal taught that the main soul correction we're all here to do is to learn emuna.

Men learn emuna (and correct their souls) via making parnassa; women learn emuna (and correct their souls) via their families.

When I try to do my husband's job, two things happen: I prevent him from learning emuna and turning to God; and I prevent myself from achieving my own soul correction, because I'm off trying to be a man, instead of being a mother and a woman.

When there are financial issues, they are ONLY coming to teach the man emuna and to get him to make teshuva. (This sounds controversial, but it's all based on Torah.)

The Gemara tells us: honour your wives and become rich. This is a big clue about what a lot of men might need to make teshuva about. Other things that can cause men big 'money' issues include a lack of modesty (including ogling other women on the internet) spilling seed deliberately, anger problems; and, of course, lack of emuna.

'Lack of emuna' is when people refuse to see God behind their financial issues, and instead blame other people for their money problems. For example, many husbands often fall into the trap of blaming their money issues on their wives for not working, or for not working enough.

The reason this doesn't work is because spiritually, women are the pipe of abundance for the home, including for finances. If we're miserable - even if we're working three jobs - our finances will be lousy. If we're happy - even if we aren't working at all - our finances will be blessed, even if there isn't a lot of money.

(This is a good time to note that 'work' is not the same as 'purpose', and for women, they can often be diametrically opposed.)

Of course, it's not 'forbidden' for a woman to work, and it's not even a bad thing, but only under the following circumstances:

She has to enjoy it enough to do it for free.

It doesn't come ahead of her children, or at least, not on a regular basis (the odd deadline, the odd 'big' push is fine, but not as a regular way of life.)

She has to WANT to be doing it, and not just doing it because her husband refuses to learn some emuna.

The waiting game

For months' now, I've been getting some version of the same message in my chats with God: "Hang on. You're nearly there. It's all going to turnaround soon, and be better than it's ever been."

I've been struggling with so many issues on so many fronts, that I'm really, really desperate to believe that it's all going to improve soon.

But then I hit a day like today, and it's like all my spiritual reserves have disappeared.

I've been having disturbing dreams the last few days, and they all have the same sort of theme: I'm homeless, I'm lost; me and my life are full of 'holes' that can't seem to be filled, I'm a stranger, an outsider, etc.

I wake up after these dreams completely drained, and then I go through the day with huge anxiety.

Dear reader, I talk to God a lot, and that's really what's been keeping me going. I *know* I'm struggling at the moment, despite all my praying and other stuff, because objectively, I have huge challenges going on in my life that I appear to be powerless to change or fix.

Whatever practical effort, or *hishtadlut*, me and my husband has tried the last two years has failed spectacularly.

There is nothing else to do except pray, and wait for God to turn things around.

Nervous breakdowns notwithstanding, I thought I was doing OK with having no income, no stability, no community, and some other excruciating tests of emuna that I can't even begin to talk about.

But my dreams are showing me otherwise.

Last night's dream was a classic: an old 'successful' friend was driving me in their car to stay with some other hugely successful people, in their enormous flat, because I was homeless and penniless.

The whole drive, I kept seeing things with holes in them - massive holes in the ground, holes in the furniture, holes in the buildings.

It sounds fairly tame as nightmares go, but I woke up feeling so despairing today, that I had to talk to God for a whole hour just to be able to get out of bed.

I feel like I've spent the best part of a decade waiting for God to rescue me from the darkness, but recently, at least in my life, it's just intensified.

What's a person to do, when they've been to Uman seven times, talked to God for hours, got blessings and advice from holy people, tried to make teshuva on everything they can think of, and still they're stuck, spiritually?

Answers on a postcard, please.

And in the meantime, I'll continue to play the waiting game.

 # School time #

We moved to Jerusalem on July 1, 2014, the day before the Israeli Government began 'Operation Protective Edge' to try to prevent the Arabs in Gaza rocketing the country every five minutes with GRAD missiles (the more sophisticated cousins of SCUDs, replete with their own GPS).

The local Arabs started rioting all around us, and I kind of felt like I'd landed in some crazy 'Nam movie, or something, between the police sirens, the rocket sirens and 'breaking news' alerts every five minutes. It was a very intense introduction to life in Jerusalem. Thankfully, that mini-war ended before Rosh Hashanah, and things seemed to calm down a little.

For about a month.

My kids now go to school in the Old City of Jerusalem. Yes, *that* Old City, where people are now getting stabbed with screwdrivers, knives, bits of rusty fencing - whatever the Arabs have to hand, basically.

Usually, someone tells me a particularly 'juicy' stabbing story five minutes after my kids were just in the same location, or are planning to go there tomorrow. My kids' friends live in the Muslim Quarter of the Old City, or in Ir David (right next to Silwan Village) or in Maalei Zeitim - a small Jewish village right next to the Mount of Olives that has its own machine-gun outpost.

This is all super-cool stuff - when it's not your kids that are going to visit these places.

But when it's your kids, what else can you do besides making sure you say Tikkun Haklali pretty much every single day, and shoving a bunch of coins in the charity box for them every time they step out the door?

Apart from one kid who lives in Har Homa, and another kid who lives in Givat Mordechai, pretty much every single one of my kids' classmates comes to school under armed guard - what's called '*levuyi*', in Hebrew.

Sometimes, when God gives me a rare moment to catch my breath, I think about the enormous bizarreness of so much of my life right now, and it almost makes me laugh: I mean, Arabs scare the pants off me! Almost as much as having to wear a tichel...

So the fact that my kids now get to school by walking through the Arab shuk in the Old City, and that all their social engagements involve being escorted by two big ex-soldier guys with guns is still something I often can't believe.

It's a constant, daily reminder that God is running the world, not me.

I'm working really hard to hand the control panel back to God at the moment, and to do my best to be happy about my present circumstances. That's the true definition of emuna: being happy with your lot.

But it's definitely easier when your kids are going to some quiet village prep school with excellent academic standards, you own your own house, your husband has a steady job, and you have maybe half a clue about what you think you're doing in life and what it's all about.

The Old City is such a holy, crazy place to be intimately involved with. On the one hand, I'm thrilled my kids are there in school, and on the other hand, I sometimes wish they were anywhere else in the country.

But then, my daughter told me an Arab stabbed some people on a bus in 'safe' Tel Aviv this morning (she has all the latest 'Arab stabbing' news, often even before Ynet), and I realised that God really is in charge.

We need to do what we need to do, and trust in God's goodness, and then let go.

We're really not in control.

Of all the lessons I've learnt from my children's school, that's probably the most important.

February 2015

//

\# "*God made prozac*" \#

The other day, I walked past a billboard in Meah Shearim for one of the local healthcare providers here in Israel, which had a big picture of a smiley chareidi doctor doing two big thumbs up. The slogan underneath read something like: "A billion children's visits to the doctor!!"

Apparently, the healthcare provider felt that this was cause for some celebration, but I walked away scratching my head.

Israel is not a big country - it's got about 6 million residents. The number of children is clearly less than that. The number of children going to this particular health care provider (probably around 50%) is even less than that.

Now, I'm not a maths whiz, but that sounds like an awful lot of sick children, too me. I mean, by the time you're taking them off to the doctor it's usually already up to a level of 'serious'.

What's going on here?

Why are there so many sick children walking around?

(Of course, I have my own ideas, but what do *you* think?)

On a separate, but related note, I was telling someone who lives in Meah Shearim about my new book which talks *tachlis* about how to keep ourselves mentally and physically healthy by getting God involved in our health.

I'm planning to do two versions - one for the 'frum' Jewish world, and one for the non-Jewish world.

She told me very candidly: "You've got an uphill struggle. Most people in the Jewish frum world will just tell you 'God made prozac, and He wants us to use it', and that's the end of the conversation."

I was a little bit shocked.

Are things really that bad? I mean, yes, God made prozac, but He also made heroin, cocaine, rocket propelled grenades, Arab terrorists, internet porn and the IRS.

If someone came up and told me 'God made heroin, and He wants me to use it to feel happy' - that argument really wouldn't fly with me.

God made EVERYTHING, in the world, absolutely everything. Our job down here is to choose between 'good' and 'bad', and between 'what God wants' and 'what God doesn't want'.

Sometimes, I can't believe the moral madness I'm trying to deal with. If I was dealing with a bunch of atheists who were big believers in the idea that 'bodies are all there is', and they were telling me this stuff, that would be one thing. But when you're dealing with the people who are meant to be the 'light unto the nations'? It's kinda depressing.

When God is out of the picture, who's to say using heroin *is* wrong? I mean, if you could get it on prescription, what's the problem? It's probably cheaper to produce and has less side effects than most of the other things being produced by Glaxo...

Sigh.

One step at a time. One day at a time.

And who knows? Maybe one day, someone in Meah Shearim will still buy my book.

Physical 'reality'

Most people, including very religious Jews, simply don't know quantum physics.

If they knew quantum physics - even the smallest little bit of it - they would know that each atom is comprised of one particle of 'stuff' to between 10,000 and 100,000 particles of space.

And what keeps all that 'space' around all that 'stuff' is light.

Everything in the physical universe, from buildings, to cars, to trees to people, including you and me, is basically made up of literally a speck of dust that's floating around in a lot of space, and light.

THAT is the physical reality of our world.

Isn't it amazing that this so closely describes Adam HaRishon, the 'Being of Light', who wore garments of revealed light before he ate from the tree of the knowledge of good and evil?

After Adam sinned, God made him and Chava different, more 'physical' garments - skin instead of light. But really? The light is still there, just a lot more hidden away.

I wish more people in the religious world would learn more quantum physics, because then it would make discussions about physical health, and souls and energy that much more straightforward.

When we relate to our bodies and our health as being purely functions of physical matter, apart from the fact that Jewishly, that idea is pure heresy, it's also completely inaccurate, according to cutting-edge science.

And if the one doesn't bother you, surely the other one should?

Getting unstuck

Yesterday, I was feeling massively 'stuck' again. I speak to a few people, and that feeling seems to be fairly widespread at the moment. It doesn't matter what the external circumstances of our lives are, how many kids, projects, jobs, achievements we're busy racking up, so many of us are still feeling kind of empty and 'stuck', wondering if we're ever going to be the people God truly designed us to be.

That is happening to me so much at the moment. No matter how much praying, how much writing, how much learning, how much reading, how much effort I make to 'do' something, I still feel pretty empty a lot of the time, like I'm not in the place I'm meant to be, internally.

I don't know how to solve this problem.

Yesterday I skipped off to the zoo to do another massive praying session. Usually, I come back from those visits feeling much calmer, happier, holier, and inspired - even if I'm still actually 'stuck'.

But that didn't happen yesterday. Yesterday, I prayed my socks off for hours, and I made a big effort to ask God to help me to be more grateful for all my blessings. I came home, and within seconds I felt the most ungrateful I'd felt for months, about everything.

"Look at my rubbish life! Look at my rubbish circumstances! I'm not earning any money! I'm just spinning my wheels! I'm a rubbish mother! I have no idea what God wants from me, or how I'm meant to be giving it to Him! I'm stuck, I'm still completely stuck!"

I was also a bit baffled: why was I having such a negative reaction *dafka* after such a big praying session? I started to think that maybe now, I was also somehow talking to God *wrong*, on top of all other things I'm apparently failing at.

Then I remembered what my rabbi recently wrote: I have to be happy, even with my

spiritual failures.

Then I remembered what another one of my rabbis recently said: when your *yetzer* drags you to those deep places of despair, if you continue to talk to God about it all, and you'll achieve a massive spiritual rectification, even if it doesn't look like that at the time.

So this is what I decided to do: I decided to thank God for my chronic, apparently incurable ingratitude and feelings of stuck-ness.

I tried it out this morning, and I could tell my *yetzer* was completely stumped. I mean, it's been beating me up for being incurably ungrateful for years. Now that I was thanking God for giving me my ingratitude issues, it couldn't really find a way to land any punches on me.

And you know what? I feel so much better! I'm still stuck, Baruch Hashem. I'm still (apparently...) incurably ungrateful. But at least now I'm feeling pretty good about it.

And that's got to count for something.

It's not a competition

You know, it's just struck me how so many of us are so busy 'competing' for attention / kudos / success / popularity etc., that it's making it really hard for us to appreciate what other people are actually trying to do to build the world. (As always, I'm talking about myself here...)

Someone just sent me a newsletter for her new website and it was beautifully done, and very colourful and professional. My first thought was: 'Wow! This looks so impressive!'

My second thought was: 'Man, I could never do something this good...'

My third thought was: 'What the heck am I saying??!?!?'

Because instead of appreciating the time and effort that had gone into my correspondent's beautiful site, my *yetzer* instead had me putting more time and effort into tearing myself down.

I had to work for a good half an hour to stop feeling like a complete loser again, and to focus on what God want me to focus on, namely, gratitude.

Whenever I get sucked into 'competing', I can't be grateful for the beautiful light others are shining into the world.

Instead of focusing on the other person's 'plus', I start obsessing over my own 'minus' again, and instead of feeling happy that there are such amazing things going on around me, I start fretting that someone else's light is somehow detracting from my own.

But it's baloney!!

Once I worked all that out, I decided I needed to call the person in question, and tell her how great her site looked. I needed to *appreciate* her time and effort, and get my own insecurities out the way. So I did.

I'm currently re-learning, for the millionth time, that it's not a competition. There is enough success / attention / kudos / appreciation / light available for everyone, and instead of worrying that I'm not 'good enough', I just need to appreciate all the good out there, and to trust that God will help me to shine my own light in whatever way it needs to happen, whenever it needs to happen.

Jerusalem past

When my family got 'frum', when I was around 16, I started reading a whole lot of biographies and stories by interesting *baal teshuvas*, or people who came back to observant Judaism. In nearly every case, Jerusalem had a starring role. People would be surfing, studying for university, back-packing in some third world country, and somehow, the call of Jerusalem would reach them, and they'd stop everything to come and answer it.

By the time they were writing their story for other *baal teshuvas* to read, it always meant that they'd got hooked on Jerusalem, on holiness, on God, on Yiddishkeit, and that now they were here to stay.

I used to get very starry-eyed about the Holy City portrayed in those books. It was a place of quiet simplicity, homemade challahs, Tzaddikim on every corner, and colourful, real people who'd sacrificed every aspect of 'normal' and 'comfortable' to follow their souls towards God.

Of course, after living in Israel for 9 1/2 years, I kind of forgot all that starry-eyed stuff, and Jerusalem became much more a place where I could find long skirts, kosher 'mehadrin' falafel and a great zoo.

When we moved here in the summer, the vision of 'Jerusalem, past' got even more blown to smithereens. My neighbours were Dutch *goyim*; the Old City was a war zone; and my own striving for spirituality got so severely curtailed it almost evaporated.

A few days' back, someone lent me a book to read called 'I remembered in the night your name', by Varda Branfman. It was a collection of short stories and poems, based around the author's experience of making teshuva in the 70s, and coming to live - where else? - In Jerusalem.

There were a couple of things that caught my attention in the book. The main one was that she was describing the holiness and simplicity of the Jerusalem neighbourhood called Geula.

I nearly fell off my chair.

Geula is a 10 minute walk from me, via Meah Shearim, and 'holy' and 'simple' are not the first words that spring to mind. Try: 'glatt pizza'; 'clothing stores'; 'hustle and bustle'; 'trendy opticians'; and 'Brooklyn Bake Shop'.

I go to Geula to spend money, and that's about it. It's always been one of the least spiritually-inspiring neighbourhoods in Jerusalem.

So I was stunned by the author's glowing description of it. Was I just not seeing all the holiness there, or has it changed beyond all recognition in the last two decades?

Varda's book reminded me of all those BT biographies I used to read, and I suddenly got a lump in my throat about 'Jerusalem, past'. I remembered how I yearned to be here, 25 years' ago, and how I was sure it was full of holy, crazy, friendly, amazing people who would invite anyone and anything for Shabbat, and literally exude 'connection to God' and spiritual inspiration.

Now I actually live here, and I wonder what happened?

Does that place still exist, and I just haven't found it yet? Or did it disappear under all the 'gashmius' and 5 star apartment complexes?

I don't know what the answer is. But it gave me renewed strength to start searching again. Jerusalem IS the holy city; even with all the face-lifts, and all the xtians, and all the politics and all the pizza, somewhere underneath all that, is a city of spiritual gold.

And now, I'm on a mission to rediscover it.

Like yourself

Have you ever had one of those days when you kind of feel like God forgot about you? Yes, He made you, He gave you life, and maybe even a husband and kids and a mortgage - but now He's busy with the civil war in Syria, or ISIS in Iraq, or the Israeli elections, and you've just kind of fallen through the gap...

I was feeling that way yesterday. I've been praying for things to turn around for ages, and they haven't (as far as I can tell) and yesterday, I was convinced that God had forgotten about me.

Where's my book deal, God? Where's my parnassa? Where's my 'success', my new house, my new car, my new outlook on life?!?!

I was really dejected, but I'd already made an arrangement to meet a friend at a Tu B'Shvat event, and I didn't want to let her down.

I got there, and a larger than life Temani grandma is running the show, making millions of pitas and telling us all about God and emuna.

Within the first five minutes, she'd already covered talking to God, doing six hours, how God answers every prayer, and the stupidity of worrying about tomorrow instead of living for today.

And if that wasn't already enough for one evening, more was still to come. She then moved on to the topic of liking ourselves, and how when we don't like ourselves, we're always looking for acknowledgement and recognition and praise from outside, and how unhealthy that is.

I sat straight up in my chair.

"Don't keep whining that no-one's praising your cookies!" she said. "If the plate's empty, it's a sign they like them. Give yourself a pat on the back, and be happy!"

As if I hadn't already realised that she'd been scripted by God to tell me exactly what I needed to hear, the Temani grandma then started listing all the weird physical symptoms she'd developed a few years' back, by getting too stressed about things instead of trusting Hashem to come through for her:

Funny eyes; weakness on one side of her body; extreme ex-haustion, etc. (i.e. all the weird physical symptoms I've also had over the past few years.)

OK, OK, I got it!

God *is* aware of what's going on with me. He's noticing every-thing. The prayers *are* all being heard, and they'll be answered in due course.

"Ein Od Milvado!" The Temani grandma yelled out, and winked at me.

I don't know if Eliyahu Hanavi ever comes back as a woman, but if yes, I think I may have seen him in action yesterday. And let me tell you, he cooks a mean pita.

A real guest

So last week, I told my husband: "*Enough of being* hermits!! We need to start inviting people for Shabbat again."

Just one problem: we don't know that many people to ask. But my husband is never one to shirk a challenge, so on Friday night he told me he'd met someone who was sleeping rough at the Kotel until he gets his *aliyah* status sorted out, and that he'd invited him for Friday night supper.

Gulp.

Let me tell you, he ended up being a very sweet, sincere guy. I was really touched by my guest's *mesirut nefesh* (self-sacrifice). He'd come to Israel on a one-way ticket with barely any money, because he got lit-up with holy enthusiasm to live a more au-thentic orthodox lifestyle, and he felt he couldn't really do that back in the States.

He'd had a quite a time of it since then, and in between grab-bing any Torah lessons at any yeshiva he could, he was trying to sort out his status as a new immigrant.

In the meantime, his money's run out, and he's sleeping rough at the Kotel with such a good grace that it's hugely embarrassing for me to remember how much I've been moaning about living somewhere *rented*, that doesn't have a bath.

After he left, I went to bed truly grateful for my bed. And my blankets. And the roof over my head.

I woke up feeling truly grateful for my bed, my blankets, my roof, my food, and my sneaky bar of hazelnut chocolate that I love eating for Shabbat breakfast.

My husband said to me later that he felt we'd just had our first ever 'real' guest for Shabbat. Sure, we've had people we don't know before, people who don't keep mitzvoth before, even people we don't like very much before - but all those people had somewhere else they could be. They had a home, an oven, an ability to make their own meals, etc.

This was the first time we ever had a 'guest' in the truest sense of the word, and it felt like a massive privilege.

Who is like your people, Hashem? Not for the first time, I felt privileged to be part of Am Yisrael. Every single one of us is so beautiful, and the more I'm looking for that diamond in every person I meet, the more God is uncovering it for me.

'Borderline idol worship'

So, I decided to get my kollel-student-almost-a-rabbi husband involved in pinning down what is halachically-acceptable, when it comes to energy medicine stuff. That was my first mistake. You see, I thought that after hearing me talk about this stuff for years, and practising it on him, repeatedly, that he actually had the first clue what Jewish energy medicine is all about.

Instead, I got this:

"How is what you're doing *Jewish*?'

What was the man talking about?!?!?

"God's in it! God's in everything I do, from start to finish! It's all about trying to connect people back to their emotions, and then back to their souls, and then back to God."

Three hours' later, I thought I'd educated him enough to let him loose calling the number of a Rav who was apparently very sympathetic and knowledgeable about energy medicine stuff.

That was my second mistake.

After 10 seconds of niceties, I heard my husband say something like this:

"So, my wife is dabbling in some borderline *avoda zara* stuff, and I just want to check it's OK."

Dear reader, I nearly strangled him.

Even with that great introduction, the Rav reassured my husband that my work with energy meridians, emotions and muscle testing was actually completely fine, halachically.

Great!

Except my husband wasn't convinced. He got off the phone muttering about not being given 'any sources' - and I suddenly realised that I am living with the world's biggest critic of Jewish energy medicine.

Hmmm.

After sulking about it for two days, I realized that God is actually doing me a massive favour here: I'm having to prove the halachic acceptability of every little thing I'm trying to do to *my own husband* before I can start really trying to roll this out into the frum world, and that's actually very helpful.

If he was even an iota less resistant, I'd have definitely gone the easier route, and stopped when we got the 'OK' from the first couple of rabbis we asked. But he's pushing me all the way to the top, halachically, to get solid answers about what energy techniques really are acceptable and spiritually-safe, and which aren't.

But tolerance still has its limits. I told my husband that if he makes one more stupid comment about Chinese Medicine being akin to black magic, I'm going to turn him into a frog. ☺

Blue sky, grey sky

As I was lying in bed on Shabbat, watching the sky alternate between a brilliant spring blue, and a gloomy, maximum-Winter grey, it struck me how the weather in this country is SOOOO holy.

In the UK, where I'm from, the sky most days is some version of grey, with the odd patch of blue showing through in between the clouds (occasionally, in the summer time...)

When I lived Montreal, a place known for its massive extremes of weather, you could certainly have a tremendously cold, but still sunny day in the middle of the snowy season; and you could also have a cloudy day in August, prior to one of Montreal's spectacular summer thunderstorms.

But what I've never seen anywhere else is a sky going from powder blue, to darkest grey, to powder blue, to darkest grey - literally changing every 10 minutes from one extreme to the other.

I was watching the heavy snow fall in Jerusalem, and interspersed with it, I was watching the sun shine out unabashed, and it took my breath away.

I could deal with the grey, snowy horrible weather so much better because I knew the sun was literally a 10 minute wait away. I could also enjoy the sun, because I knew that we've had enough rainfall this year to last us a decade (but that won't stop them printing 'drought imminent' stories again next year, as soon as we get past Pesach.)

As I lay there, looking at the sky, I realized God was given me a *mashaal*, or an allegory for life, especially life in Israel, and especially, my life at the moment.

I've hit every 'grey' extreme going the last few months. I've had days when I literally felt like I couldn't take it anymore, and I felt like I was going to explode, or break into pieces, if something didn't change, pronto.

And then, the clouds parted, and I'd feel so much better, and calmer, and even a little bit happy again. I was back in my 'blue sky' mind-set. And then 10 minutes later, the freezing wind and hail and snow showed up again, figuratively speaking.

The other day, I was trying to work out what's been the most difficult thing to deal with the last few years, and what came through loud and clear was 'uncertainty'. Nothing in my life is certain. Not only that, my life, my attitude, my outlook, can flip from stormiest grey to sunniest blue in a second - and then flip back again in another second.

It's enough to drive you bonkers.

But then, I looked at the sky on Shabbat, and I saw that this uncertainty is actually a blessing, in many ways, because it's hiding the certainty of God, and His kindness, and the way He's directing the world and my life.

After half an hour, I really got that God is controlling the extreme weather; God is flipping the switch; God is tipping things from grey to blue, and back again. When I need grey, I'll get it. When I need blue, I'll get it - and things will change according to what God decides is best for me.

And that's for certain.

So like I said, even the weather in Israel is holy, and can teach us some profound lessons about how God is in charge of everything. We just have to take that half an hour, or five minutes, or two seconds to stay still, sit quiet, and try to work out the message He's hiding in everything, including the freak weather.

Feeling the heat

Half an hour before my youngest was set to walk (by herself) to the Old City, for her standard Shabbat afternoon youth group gathering, she 'casually' mentioned, by the way, that a few people got stabbed and / or run over again close by, in the last couple of days.

I don't listen to the news, thank God, so my children are the nearest I get to CNN, and even their occasional broadcasts are enough to give me palpitations.

You know, of all the challenging things my move to Jerusalem engendered, the ongoing Arab violence has been by far the biggest test of emuna.

For a couple of months it got kind of 'normal' around here, and I stopped being so anal about praying on my children every time they left home that they should return safely, or putting money in my charity box for them *immediately* they left the house.

It was nice, albeit I can see that God gets so much more real for me, and for them, when we start hearing more reports of an Ahmed going crazy with a big knife down by the Damascus Gate again.

Discomfort tends to bring out the best in us, doesn't it? Much as I hate that feeling of repressed panic, it motivates me like nothing else to turn to God, and to ask for His help.

"God, please look after my kids. Bring them back safely. Make it that the Arabs shouldn't even notice them. In fact, no man should even so much as look at them, for at least another four years..."

As we head into Spring after what seems like the longest, wettest, coldest winter I've experienced in the almost 10 years I've lived in Israel, part of me is ready for it to start heating-up again, weather-wise.

It could be that other things are also starting to heat-up again, although I really, really hope they're not.

People getting stabbed on the doorstep is a very uncomfortable feeling. It makes me realise all over again how fragile life really is, and how grateful I need to be for so many things - like my kids, like my husband - that it's so easy to take for granted. Nothing bursts my 'feeling secure' bubble as fast, or as effectively, than Ahmed the wannabe stabber.

But maybe, that's the point.

Swallowing my pride

In the last place I lived, I prided myself on being pretty darned frum. I tried not to talk to men I wasn't married to; I tried to wear the longest skirts I could find; I was super-proud of the fact I didn't have internet in the house, and barely any secular literature (apart from what my kids were sneaking home from the library...)

OOO-wah, I was *religious*.

One of the things that meant is that I was continually turning my nose up at my daughters' choice of youth group. In my old village, we were really spoilt for choice. There was Bnei Akiva (mixed crowd, tight short skirts, definitely NOT for us...) There was Ezra (technically more 'separate', but still with some mixing of the genders that caused me more than a little discomfort...) And then, there was Ariel (only for the 'real frummers', according to my daughters, but my idea of youth group Heaven, because they organised their activities around the *yahrtzeits* of dead holy people...)

My kids went to Ezra (like all of their friends) and I tutted about it to myself, but still felt morally superior, because at least it wasn't *Bnei Akiva!*

As usual, God knew exactly how to take me down a notch or two. We got to Jerusalem, and in the area where we live, the only youth group in town (unless you were a Beis Yaacov girl) was Bnei Akiva.

Hmmm.

God softened me up for two whole months before I finally agreed to my girls going to it. Firstly, they were so miserable and lonely on Shabbat with no friends, that I was genuinely starting to worry that they'd go right off the whole idea of 'Shabbat' unless we could find them some company, pronto.

Secondly, I discovered that this Bnei Akiva was much more serious and 'religious' than the one in my old village: girls and boys were STRICTLY separated, and you wouldn't get jeered at for owning a skirt that came past your knees.

My girls tried to reassure me: "Ima, this is the most *dossi* (Hebrew slang for super-religious) Bnei Akiva in the whole country!" they told me.

Still, Bnei Akiva was Bnei Akiva...

With heavy heart, I told my girls they could go, and I mentally wiped about 300 hundred 'frum girl' Brownie points off my spiritual stash.

"God, better Bnei Akiva and happy girls than no Bnei Akiva and kids who could end up not wanting to keep Shabbat any more..."

But I wasn't 100% convinced- until last week.

Last week, my oldest was in a Bnei Akiva acting extravaganza along with 15 of her female friends - and it was an amazing experience. The event took place in a synagogue tucked away behind the Kotel (in the Muslim Quarter of the Old City) - and I actually got really emotional watching them all up on stage (and not for the same reasons I usually get 'emotional' at these types of things.)

Instead of feeling uncomfortable / bored / claustrophobic / brain-dead, I actually felt really uplifted and part of something beautiful. Maybe it was the holy atmosphere, literally five seconds' away from the Kotel. Maybe, it was seeing all the beautiful young actresses, working together as a team. Maybe, it was the true story they were acting out about Lebanese Jews trying to get to Israel.

Who knows?

All I can tell you, is that I came away from that evening thanking God that my daughters were in Bnei Akiva, at least this super-dossi branch of it.

Not in a million years did I ever think I would be writing that, or feeling those sentiments. But not for the first time, God is teaching me that when I get my false pride and holier-than-thou rubbish out the way, I can see so much more beauty in the world.

The Grinch who stole Purim

So, it's Purim time again, and instead of feeling uplifted and full of shining faith, joy and emuna, I'm feeling pretty flat this year. If you've been following my blog for a while, you'll know that's not a new development. Every single 'Adar' for the last seven years', or so, has been extremely challenging for me, and the polar opposite of the 'simcha-fest' Purim is so often made out to be.

One year, I was living in a village where one of the other families had their son murdered in the Rosh Chodesh Adar massacre at the Mercaz HaRav Yeshiva. Another Purim, there was a rainstorm of biblical proportions on the day itself, which fused both my ovens (before I'd cooked the Purim Seuda...) and completely flooded my upstairs landing.

Last year, I broke my toe on Rosh Chodesh Adar, and bizarrely spent the whole of Purim feeling the most miserable and broken I'd probably ever felt in my life.

This Rosh Chodesh Adar rolled around - and practically the minute night fell, I started to feel inexplicably weak, sick and very despairing and miserable.

I took to my bed trying not to panic that I'd been struck by the Bubonic Plague, or something, and then I remembered it was Rosh Chodesh Adar. Ah! That explains everything...

It took me a few days to recover and not feel so inexplicably shaky and fragile - just in time to go shopping for my daughters' Purim outfits. One daughter was being all flippant and 'teenage' about the whole dressing up thing, and went straight for all the most horrible, gaudy lipsticks she could find.

"What are you dressing up as? A drag queen?"

That's what I wanted to ask her, but instead, I bit my lip and smiled my fake smile, as yet another packet of tiger-striped false fingernails made it into my basket. Thank God she only dresses like that once a year.

The other daughter had a nervous breakdown trying to decide between being an Egyptian, a Greek Sylph, or Pocahontas (great, at least one of them wasn't directly connected to idol worship and a culture that revelled in killing the Jews...)

I can't tell you how high our collective stress level rose. Finally, we went to a different shop, and she settled on the Flamenco Dancer outfit (after long negotiations about HAVING to wear a long top and skirt underneath it all times.)

But the Purim revelry wasn't over yet: next on the list of super-stressful, expensive and pretty pointless things was *mishloach manot*.

For every kid in the class. Twice over. Even though it wasn't even actually Purim yet. Even though technically, packets of bamba, gummy worms and chocolate bars don't even really count as a proper *mishloach manot*.

Yet again, stress levels rose throughout the Levy household as my kids agonised over the contents, over the packaging, over whether their mishloach manot were '*shavey*' enough (Hebrew for 'worth even getting').

All this left me pondering Purim, and the true meaning of the festival. Purim is that time when everything can flip around, when we can truly see God's hand in our life, where we can achieve the most amazing miracles with our prayers.

But it all seemed to have got lost again, under wrappings of cellophane, cheap, tarty costumes and a sense of enormous motherly-overwhelm.

God, is this *really* how You want Purim to be, or has it got co-opted by the Evil Inclination?

I don't know, but in the meantime, this is what I'm going to do on the actual day itself (God willing): I'm going to put on my (very simple) cat mask; I'm going to eat a (very simple) baked salmon, with just my family; I'm going to drink just enough wine until I have no idea what's good or what's bad anymore (and believe me, I'm pretty much there even without the alcohol); and I'm asking God to shine His light into the madness of this world, as sometimes I feel I just can't take it anymore.

That's it!

I know, it's not very 'festive', is it? What can I tell you? For all the PR and all the hype, I find Purim to be one of the most serious, introspective and challenging holidays of the whole year. And maybe I've got that backwards and upside-down, but that's also in keeping with the spirit of the day.

Each year, I find myself asking the same question again: "God, is this *really* how You want my Purim to be?" And I suspect I'm not alone.

Turn it all around

In Chassidut generally, and Breslev tradition specifically, Purim is the unofficial spiritual beginning of the year. However it goes on Purim, that kind of sets the tone for the year. When you enjoy Purim as much as I do, that's a pretty scary thought.

This year, our first in the holy city of Jerusalem, we had the additional challenge of celebrating Shushan Purim on Friday, just before Shabbat came in. I was convinced it was all going to turn out to be a complete disaster, and initially, I seemed to be right.

For the last six years, God's helped me to wake up around midnight on Purim night, to do an hour of praying. It's meant to be the most powerful '*et ratzon*' or favourable time of the whole year, and as usual, I had a whole, massive list of things to pray on.

This year, I simply couldn't wake up. I woke up for about three minutes, mumbled something (I don't even remember what), then conked out again, until my regular morning wake-up call.

Not a great start.

The Megilla reading was OK, except I couldn't figure out how to wear my cat mask over my glasses without giving myself a migraine, and I couldn't use my specially bought 'grogger', as stamping on Haman was banned at that particular shul.

But I still got the mitzvah done, however colourlessly.

I came home to find my husband in a pretty bad mood, for no obvious reason - and I went berserk at him. I think it's become a tradition in our family for me and my husband to have a massive fight on Purim, and this year was no different.

I started chewing him out, big time, for his 'negative' attitude and miserable behaviour, and he stomped off, furious, to deliver the *mishloach manot* we'd got for his two main Rabbanim, at the yeshiva.

Great! Happy Purim. What a wonderful blueprint to have created for the rest of the year.

Thank God for my kids. They swung into gear and decided to try to repair the festive atmosphere a bit by making pancakes to give all the neighbours in my building, as I got the food cooked for the Purim seuda and Shabbat meal. I cheered up a bit.

An hour later, my husband came home a changed man. He'd got blessings from both his rabbis, and let me tell you, they worked.

He was the happiest I'd seen him in years. Together, we went to deliver our pancakes and juice to the neighbours, and just as we got to one flat, the wife burst into the door, and started screaming blue murder at her husband.

The traditional Purim fight.

My husband glanced at me, smirked, and said: "I see I got off lightly..."

We came home to a text message from a friend, who'd decided last minute to join us for our Purim seuda as she'd just moved house and hadn't managed to pull things together. I was so pleased to have guests, especially such laid-back guests that didn't require any more effort or cooking.

The meal was relatively quiet, relatively fast, and relatively sober, as we had Shabbat coming in a couple of hours - but it was probably the nicest Purim seuda we ever had.

Later that night, I sat by the Kotel watching the people praying, dancing, and singing Shabbat songs (interspersed with Eyal Golan), and I felt so blessed to be there.

In the space of 12 hours, I'd gone from feeling so cynical, down and despairing of my husband ever getting his act together, to seeing everything turn around for the best.

A true Purim miracle.

My tips for next year are this:

1. Get your husband to take *mishloach manot* to the biggest rabbis you can get access to

2. Encourage him to get a blessing from said big rabbis

3. Don't let him in to the house until he's done 1) and 2) above. That's it!

May we all be blessed with the most joyous, happy year, and may all our hurts dissolve, all our problems disappear, and our husbands all cheer up. Amen v'amen.

Why I love living in Israel, part 69494949

Living in Jerusalem has some disadvantages, which you could sum up like this: crazy people all over the place; Arabs; crazily-expensive apartments; and noise pollution. Like, the wailing of the muezzin from the local mosque; the local art students playing Queen loud enough to perforate your eardrums; white trash neighbours screaming blue murder at each other; sirens, etc. etc.

BUT - living in Jerusalem also has a whole bunch of advantages, too.

I was just walking home now from Machane Yehuda, Jerusalem's colourful, larger-than-life outdoor fruit and veg market, and on the way I went down Ben Yehuda street, and through what's affectionately known by the locals as 'Crack Square'.

Often, you'll find the most amazingly talented Russian musicians busking there, or some sort of 'artistic' demonstration going on. One time I walked past Crack Square and the whole floor was covered in big Stars of David, carefully crafted from empty beer bottles.

Today, I walked past it to find a spontaneous frum man dance party going on.

I have no idea how, where, why, what, all I can tell you is that around 200 'religious' men of various ages and kippa denominations were doing a synchronised dance to Shwekey.

It lasted all of a glorious 4 minutes, and then the group broke up and everyone went off to do their pre-Purim errands.

I came away a bit perplexed - how did they manage to get 200 people with 'Y' chromosomes to spontaneously do the same moves? - and absolutely thrilled that God sends me this crazy stuff to spice up my life, when I'm on the way home to make an otherwise boring supper for my family.

Where else but in Israel?

Nowhere.

Election, anybody?

So, me being the least 'connected' person I know, at least in terms of news and media, I had a shock when someone told me this Tuesday is Election Day in Israel.

Is it? Already? Didn't they just have one a couple of years' ago?

Apparently, yes, yes and yes. But someone told me a few years' ago that Israelis just love elections, as it gives them another free day off to go and take their BBQ somewhere and start grilling steaks.

So here we are, at my 5th or 6th Israeli election day in barely 10 years, and I'm sure you're dying to ask me the question of questions: who am I voting for?

I'm voting for the same people I voted for last time around: Precisely No-one.

I like Precisely No-one for a few reasons: Firstly, you don't vote in some uber-hawkish right wing PM who then promptly dismantles half the country and gives it back to the Arabs.

Also, you don't vote in some uber-liberal lefty who campaigns on a platform of giving the whole country back to the UN, as they anyway are planning on retiring to America, but who then ends up fighting a couple of serious wars.

When I vote for Precisely No-one, I'm also avoiding the pitfalls of electing frauds, gangsters, liars, mass-murderers, mafia king-pins and people with *very* scary-looking official photographs.

And to top it all off, it's also means I don't fall out with my neighbours over who I'm actually voting for. Magic.

I know some people think it's a civic duty to participate in elections. I also used to think that way, until I read something in the Gemara that explained that God holds the heart of kings in His hand. What that means *tachlis* is that whoever you vote for in the elections, Hashem is going to decide how they are actually going to behave in office.

If Am Yisrael is worthy, we can vote in the biggest waste-of-space and he'll end up actually doing a pretty good job for us. And the opposite is also true.

So if we really want to see 'peace in our time' and 'secure borders' and a 'thriving economy' and 'more opportunities for our youth' and whatever else they're all busy promising us, the best plan would be to chuck our voting ticket in the bin, and then take the hour it would take us to do our civic duty to go to a field somewhere, and go and talk to God instead.

If we all did that this Tuesday, we'd get Moshiach and royal monarchy pronto, which isn't exactly *democratic*, but still sounds pretty darned good to me, as options for ruling the country go.

 # It doesn't have to be perfect #

I tried my hand at podcasting a little while ago, and someone emailed me to let me know that at the end, you can hear my phone ringing, and then me actually answering it, in the extra second it took for my recording-thingy to switch off.

Shockingly unprofessional!

And also great, because one of the things I really want to do is to start setting the bar so much lower for us all. If I waited until I could do all this stuff perfectly, I'd never do anything, because who can do it 'perfectly', at least initially?

It's the same thing with absolutely everything I've been busy with the last few months.

When I started my Emunaroma blog up, I had no idea how to sort out the technical aspects of a blog, or even if I was going to have enough to talk about every week.

I prayed on it (which is the big key to getting anything to move), I asked God to help me, and He sent me...my husband! (See, they are sometimes useful) who told me about a great website builder he'd just found.

I got my first website set up in 2 hours. Was it perfect? No. Did it do the job? It sure did!

Over the months, I've tweaked, rearranged, and learnt a few more things, nearly all of which have started off incredibly imperfect.

Then, I got a bee in my bonnet about finishing my book. Again, I could have drafted and redrafted until it was perfect (and probably died in the attempt...) but I decided to pray on it, ask God for help, and then just take the plunge and start sending the manuscript out to friends for comments, in all its imperfection.

That was a great decision - I got a lot of very useful feedback that helped me reshape the whole book, rewrite it in less than a month, and move on to the next stage of trying to find an agent.

The latest draft is 99% done. I'm sending out my query letters to literary agents already, because (as I keep mentioning) IT DOESN'T HAVE TO BE PERFECT.

My lack of perfection is becoming my hallmark: you'll find it all over my website, all over my podcasts, all over my books, and certainly in every area of my life.

My bathroom is imperfectly spotless, my cooking is imperfectly tasteless and boring (at least, sometimes), my dishes often stack up in the sink for days, my attempts to be a good mother are usually half-baked, and my efforts to make challah are SO imperfect that it deserves a whole chapter of its own, to try and do it justice.

But you know what? I love all my imperfection! I'd much rather a great podcast with an imperfect ending (because my recording studio is my living room) than no podcast at all.

And usually, that's the choice we're all actually faced with: imperfect reality, or perfect make-believe.

So whatever it is you're procrastinating about, or sitting on, or not believing in yourself enough about - pray on it, ask God for help and take the plunge, imperfectly.

Anyway, the process is all we've really got because the outcome is 100% up to God. It may not be perfect, but it's SOME-THING, it's tangible, it's real, and you'll feel so good that you put some of your own unique light out there into the world, however imperfectly it ultimately came out.

Old banger

When I was growing up, my dad had a penchant for buying clapped-out pieces of junk with tyres, and trying to fix them. Now, my dad was very handy under the bonnet, and I spent many a long Saturday afternoon I spent waiting in the car, bored out of my mind, while my dad crow-barred a carburettor out of some matching piece of junk-on-wheels at the local breakers' yard.

Those cars worked pretty well, most of the time. When they didn't - it was a horrendous nightmare, at least for a super-self-conscious teenager. It's bad enough being seen out with your family under any circumstances when you hit 14, but being seen pushing your family car back up the road to your house (for the 8th time that week) is a whole different order of embarrassing.

As a result of my teenage car trauma, I made a very firm decision to ONLY buy new cars, when I grew up. And for the first 13 or so years' of car ownership, I stuck to it. Whenever a car approached its third birthday, I'd offload it and buy a new one. They were never fancy. I'm not a big car person, so I didn't care so much for flash or big, I just wanted simple, reliable and *new.*

The plan worked flawlessly until I got to Israel and our finances fell down a black hole. We bought a new car nine years' ago - and we've still got it. That by itself is actually an open miracle, as the car's been in at least one serious accident, and has endured innumerable other scrapes and minor bashes.

The car door creaks very loudly when you open it, a reminder of my serious car crash in Netivot, a couple of years' ago. The windscreen wipers also squeak, incessantly, so I ration their use to one swish every minute, unless it's seriously torrential rain. The beeping thingy that tells you that you left your lights on packed up four years' ago, which means we've had quite a few 'flat battery' episodes as a result.

All the internal lighting on the dashboard has died a death; I've replaced the tyres so many times I should get a set free soon; and in some senses my car's had so many parts replaced it may technically now be collectively less than three years old.

But the facts are still the facts: I'm driving an old banger.

My teenaged self would be horrified. My adult self is learning, yet again, that blessings can sometimes come in very strange packaging. I never worry about my car getting scraped, bumped or scratched. I usually leave it unlocked because I know no thief could try to steal it without waking the whole neighbourhood up when they open the squeaky door.

I clean it once - for Pesach - and then it doesn't even cross my radar for another 12 months. My kids can let all sorts of things mould and decompose in the back and (unless it really stinks) - I don't even notice. If I had a new car, I'd be far more anxious, cagey and critical of what was going on in and around it.

And wonders of wonders: it's still reliable. It's been in the garage far less than other people's much newer, more expensive cars. My husband has a theory that the car has lasted so long, and so well, because it's visited a lot of holy gravesites and is officially a four-wheeled pilgrim.

Nevertheless, it's still about 580 years old, in car years, and I'd like to give it an honourable retirement soon.

I've told God that I've got the message, and I no longer need to be hysterical about having an old car. That part of me got fixed, I promise. I hope He believes me. My daughter has plans to go to high school somewhere near Eilat, and even for someone who's used to pushing their car back home, that's a longggg way back.

From slavery to emancipation

Slavery is always a hot topic when Seder night rolls around again. For a start, the Haggadah is egging us on, and encouraging us to remember what it was like to be a slave in Egypt, and to remember how God redeemed us.

Unless you have the brilliant (but slightly gory...) pictures of the Gadi Pollack Haggadah to inspire you and transport you back to ancient Egypt, it can be pretty hard to imagine what that slavery was really like.

Or so you'd think.

But the truth is, we actually don't need a lot of imagination to get back there, because most of us are reliving the Egyptian experience right now. Of course, you hopefully aren't bricking your child into your garden wall (although that does sound kinda tempting to the mother of teenagers...); and your boss lets you take Yom Tov off as unpaid leave; and you have a great career, and a great life, and a lovely home.

So you're probably wondering 'where's the similarity?!?'

In our materialistic world, we get so caught up in how things *look* that we all too often overlook how things really *feel*. Today, it all *looks* great. But how does it *feel*? Do you feel like a free person, or do you feel enslaved to your job, your mortgage, or your i-Phone?

Our Sages teach that the Egyptian exile was the blueprint for every subsequent exile and redemption of the Jewish people, so let's go pick up some clues to see how what was happening then is still playing out in our own lives.

> **Clue 1: People were so stressed and miserable, they literally couldn't breathe (the** *kotzer ruach* **phenomenon.)**

Today, we see exactly the same phenomenon.

Asthma and breathing difficulties are at record levels, but even if our airways are physically unobstructed, most of us are still not breathing anywhere near as deeply or as healthily as we could be. We breathe through our mouths; we take shallow breaths; we don't have the time to really exhale....And all these things have spiritual, emotional and physical consequences.

It's a chicken-and-an-egg thing: we feel stressed, anxious, nervous, fearful etc., so we hold our breath. Holding our breath causes us to feel even more stressed, anxious, nervous, fearful etc. When people are holding their breath, they can't speak. They can't cry. They can't shout. They can't communicate. They can't pray, and call out to God to help them. Does this sound familiar to anyone?

> **Clue 2: Gender Role-reversals.**

Those crafty Egyptians were the original womens'-libbers. They had women running board meetings, and organising the local brick-building co-operatives, while the men were stuck at home making the beds and trying to look after the kids.

What's wrong with that, you might ask? Sounds great!

Well, women need high levels of the hormone oxytocin to feel good, relaxed and happy.

Oxytocin is produced by engaging in nurturing, caring, social activities, like looking after your kids, having a bubble bath and sharing a deep conversation with someone you care about. Oxytocin gets completely wiped out by the sort of testosterone-inducing stress you encounter in the hard-nosed world of work.

On the male side of the equation, they feel good, happy and relaxed when they have enough testosterone flowing through their veins. Testosterone gets produced by activities that involve deadlines, urgency, problem solving and achieving specific goals - and not by babysitting and doing the dishes.

When a man gets too much oxytocin and not enough testosterone, they get stressed and miserable. When a woman gets too much testosterone and not enough oxytocin, they get stressed and miserable. Now, you can start to see the evil genius of the Egyptians. And again, doesn't this sound all too familiar in today's world?

The last clue, Clue 3: Men who just couldn't take it anymore.

In Egypt, the men gave up. Their huge anxiety over making a living had crushed them to such a point that all they wanted to do was to spend their evenings surfing the internet or crashing out in front of the TV.

Moshe Rabbenu showed up ready to redeem the Jewish people, and the men didn't want to hear. They'd stopped believing in themselves, and in their ability to change, and to be happy, and to be truly emancipated. They even convinced themselves that they were *happy* being miserably enslaved, and got really shirty when anyone tried to convince them otherwise.

Do you know who saved the day, and turned the situation around? The women.

The women went out to the field, and up to their husband's offices, and told them: "Enough running away from yourself and from me and from God and from freedom!

Put down your i-Phone, and start believing in yourself again! You're a Jew, not a robot! I'm not going to give up on you, and I'm not going to let you give up on yourself, either! God's waiting to redeem us! Get with the program!"

They didn't nag (much...) or rant (excessively...) or berate or criticise (unfairly...). They just bludgeoned their husbands into submission with the power of prayer, and with a lot of unconditional love and hope. And today, God's waiting for us to do the same.

We don't have to go back 3,300 years and try to picture what it was like building a pyramid. Just go back a day, or a week, or a month, and remember how lonely, stressed, scared and anxious you felt. How worried you are, secretly, about your husband, and your kids; how much you really want your life to change, and to flourish and to blossom.

How desperate you are to really serve Hashem, happily, as a Jew.

And then go and talk to God about it all. The women got us out of Egypt, and they'll get us out of this exile, too.

The gauge of madness

As has become my habit, I went down to the Kotel Friday night, to do a bit of praying. Usually, I spend half an hour watching the dancing, singing young women, and feeling pretty privileged, before I go and sit at the back of the Plaza, to wait for my husband to show up.

There's always a lot of interesting stuff going on back there, like wedding parties from South Africa, Birthright groups, or barmitzvah tour parties from Argentina. Last week, the colour at the Kotel was provided by a bunch of uber-secular Israel teenagers, who have started showing up on Friday nights on a fairly regular basis.

I think there's some new organisation schlepping all these kids to Jerusalem for 'The Wall Experience' from Haifa, and Hod HaSharon, and who knows where else. So anyway, like you'd expect, these secular teenagers dig the Kotel scene for about five minutes, and then get really bored and hang out at the back of the Plaza, waiting for their guide to show up and schlep them somewhere else.

While they're waiting they joke around, dance a bit, play 'slapping' games - the usual stuff. This week, I was watching a crowd of teens doing all of the above when one really caught my eye. He was a very good-looking teen, very friendly, very outgoing.

There was just one problem: he had massive holes in his ears, where his earlobes should be.

Eeuwwwww! Yuk! What's with that?

I couldn't take my eyes off his 'gauges', as I've learned these massive ear-hole making things are called, and in my heart I grieved for this kid, and his mother.

I mean, she can't have liked it when her son showed up looking like a bad Salvador Dali painting.

The problem I have with gauges, similar to the problem I have with tattoos, is that I just can't believe that people want to permanently mutilate themselves. I mean, it sounds cool when you're 16, but I'm willing to bet a lot of money that when that kid is 30 and trying to get a job, the gauges are not going to be top of his list of the 'best decisions I ever made'.

How can someone decide that they're ALWAYS going to want big holes in their ears?

Or a big tattoo of Elvis on their bicep? It seems to be an act of quiet, desperate, stagnation.

And nothing kills the spirit faster than desperation and stagnation.

Sure, I know that's not how the 16 year old sees it. The 16 year old thinks he looks cool, in that 'ancient African tribesman' sort of way. For now.

On the way home, I asked my kids what they thought about the 'gauge of madness', and they also made appropriate puking noises. Thank God for that. The oldest one is still going on about getting a second ear piercing and dying her hair blue, which until I saw the 'gauge of madness' was pretty annoying.

Now? I think I got off lightly...

Divine providence

Of all the super-annoying discussions I've had down the years (and believe me, there's been thousands of them) - pretty much top of the list is the following statement:

"We can never know the reasons why God does what He does."

At first blush, it sounds reasonable, doesn't it? I mean, how can us small human beings understand anything about God, and how He's running the world? He's so big, and omnipotent and so, well, Divine, and we? Well, we're not.

But the problem with this statement is that it goes directly contrary to an authentic Jewish view of Divine Providence. The Rambam in his famous 13 Principles of Faith states that: 'God did, does and will do everything'. Jewishly, God isn't the main player in town, He's the ONLY player in town.

Every little thing that happens to us is a result of Divine Providence. If we get a parking spot, or fail to find one - that's God. If we are earning a fortune or struggling to put food on the table - that's God. If we're fit and healthy, or struggling with all sorts of health issues, God forbid, that's God.

What does all this mean? And what does it have to do with the statement that 'we can never know the reasons why God does what He does?'

Well, it's like this: God is doing everything, and everything He's doing is purposeful. It all has a meaning, a reason, a purpose, and what might that purpose be? Simple: He wants us to work on all our bad character traits, and to fix our souls.

If we spill ketchup on our new suit - that's a hint from God about something that we need to look at, ponder, and work on in ourselves.

If we have a massive argument with our spouse - ditto.

If the bank forecloses on our house - still ditto.

None of these things are random. They are all messages from God about what particular thing He wants us to work on next. Of course, it's not always so easy to work out the messages, and without regular talking to God sessions, it can be even more challenging.

But when you talk to God on a regular basis, and when you really try to listen to Him, you'll work out most of the clues, most of the time.

Strangely, a lot of people don't like to hear that. They like to pretend that everything that's happening to them is random, by chance, or 'fate', because that way, they don't have to change, or face-up to any uncomfortable truths about themselves and their behaviour.

I understand that, I really do. I've sometimes also been tempted to take that route myself, but God hasn't let me. Every time I stuck my head in the sand and pretended that 'we can never know the reasons why God does what He does', God has whacked up the heat, and sent me an even bigger, clearer message that I simply couldn't continue to ignore.

And the truth is, He actually does this for most of us. The small spat with our spouse turns into a full-blown war; the small problem with our kid turns into a serious issue in school; the minor health issue deteriorates into something pretty serious, God forbid.

At that point, we can continue to say 'we can never know the reasons why God does what He does', or we can bite the bullet and ask God to show us what's going on. As soon as we take that option, we've already solved more than half the problem.

I have had so many massive, practically unsolvable problems that turned around in record time, once I got the message and started working on whatever it was God wanted me to look at.

Do I know why I had a two-year-long slug festival in my old house in the UK, or why so many of my toilets have seriously malfunctioned in every single house that I've lived in? Nope. But I now have a pretty good idea about why my kids were so miserable a few years' back when I was working all the time, and why so many of my relationships soured, and why my finances had to go into melt-down.

It's true we can't know *everything* about why God does what He does. But we can still all know more than enough to figure out what we probably need to work on, and fix. But only if we're willing to admit that we're not yet perfect.

To be an individual – dealing with teens

Like many of us, my friend Miriam only became an observant Jew in her late thirties. Before that, she and her husband ate shrimp, watched movies, and wore bikinis. (OK, her husband didn't actually do *that*...) But, they did live a very secular, hedonistic lifestyle.

Then they got *frum*, and everything changed.

Everything was great, until Miriam's teenage kid came to her one day and told her that he didn't want to keep Shabbat anymore. Miriam was stunned, disappointed and hurt. She was also furious. After all the sacrifices that she and her husband had made to return to Judaism, how could her son be so ungrateful, shallow and superficial as to turn his back on it all?!

After all, he'd been given every advantage, Jewishly. He'd been sent to Jewish school, he knew Hebrew, he was comfortable going to shul and eating kosher, and he had a ton of 'frum' friends to hang out with.

For weeks, the tension stated building up at home, until one Friday night, after a particular tense face-off with her son, Miriam's reserve finally cracked. She started saying the most horrible, terrible things to her wayward teen, at full volume, in front of her husband the rest of the kids.

The son visibly blanched, and stalked off to his room, slamming the door loudly behind him.

"Great!" Miriam started ranting. "He's going to listen to music, and smoke, and break Shabbat and do all the other things that deadbeats like him do!"

The other children looked at her, shocked, and now it was Miriam's turn to visibly blanch and stalk off to her own room, slamming the door loudly behind her.

Then the internal fight of the century began in Miriam's soul:

"Stuff him, the ungrateful so-and-so! I give up. I can't help this kid. He's so broken and I just can't fix him. I just want to go to sleep, and forget all about him..."

But Miriam's soul wouldn't let her. As she lay there, her soul started prompting her to go and fix the mess that was being made.

"I can't!" she remonstrated.

"But you must..." her soul replied." He's no worse than you were at his age. And in many ways, he's still so much better."

After half an hour, Miriam swallowed her pride and went to visit her son, who was angrily staring at the wall, lying on his bed, and pretending not to see her.

Miriam apologised. Miriam told her son that she loved him. Miriam took a deep breath, and told her son that she wanted to hear his side. To hear what he really thought, and to find out why Shabbat was so hard for him.

After five minutes, her son finally softened up and started to talk a little. Miriam held her tongue, asked God to give her strength and patience, and just listened.

Her son explained that *he* wasn't *them*. He was desperate to be an individual. To find his own path in life.

"You got to wherever you got to, but you're 46, and I'm only 15," he said mournfully. "You can't expect me to get to where you are. I need to make my own mistakes."

Painful as it was to hear, Miriam felt in the depth of her soul that her son was right. Sobbing, she reached over to hug him, then left the room.

Later on, after a long, intense session of talking to God about it all, Miriam realised that God has infinite patience for people. Yes, she didn't want her son to make the same mistakes she had. She wanted him to live a good, happy, spiritual, 'perfect' life.

But God showed her that sometimes, for some souls, that can only be earned by experience, and not acquired for free.

God also reassured her that as long as she continued to pray for her son and to see the good in him, he wouldn't go too far away. Sooner or later, he'd come back - to God, to observant Judaism, to Miriam.

And when he did, Miriam knew he'd be better, wiser, and happier, and most importantly of all, he'd truly be *him.*

Shiloh revisited

The ancient location of Shiloh, in the Shomron, is where the first Mishkan, or Tabernacle, stood for 367 years, before the Philistines came and destroyed it.

Joshua ben Nun picked the spot, and many amazing stories from the bible occurred there, most notably the story of Chana, the barren wife, and her prayer that God should grant her children.

God answered Chana's prayer, and sent her the prophet Samuel, along with four other kids.

Shiloh is the place where Samuel served out his apprenticeship to Eli, the High Priest. Samuel famously heard God calling to him in Shiloh when he was still a young boy, which cemented his position as one of the Nation of Israel's foremost spiritual leaders.

The first time I went to Shiloh was about 7 years' ago, and I loved it. I'm a huge history buff, and the idea of walking on the same ground as Joshua, Samuel and Chana thrilled me to the core.

Seven years' ago, I also had another strong motivation for visiting Shiloh: I wanted God to do a repeat performance, and to answer my prayers to have more children.

Fast-forward to Pesach 2015, and we decided to go to Shiloh over Chol HaMoed, as they do one of the best family day outs in Israel.

I could go and look at all the ancient, 'boring' stones, while my kids biked around, made mosaics and wove themselves bracelets.

We got there, and the weather was gorgeous: a perfect, sunny cloudless sky, but with a strong breeze, so you didn't feel you were baking alive in your own skin. Israel in spring is always beautiful, but the Shomron takes it up a level. Everywhere we looked, there were natural spring flowers, trees in bloom and green mountains (plus massive road signs for the 'LadyPal' account at the Palestinian Bank, in Arabic.)

The kids went off to do their thing, and me and my husband wandered up to the site of the ancient tabernacle. On the way, there were guides stationed every few metres, to tell you a bit more of the story of ancient Shiloh.

We got to the site of the tabernacle, and there was a bloke with a guitar, seated next to a huge canvas screen that had Chana's prayer printed on it.

The bloke started singing the prayer that many Jewish mothers say when they light candles on Friday night, asking God to grant them children who will stick to the path of Torah, and be beacons of spiritual light in a world of darkness - and out of the blue, I suddenly got all choked up.

You see, I'd forgotten about all the prayers I'd offered up to have more kids. The last few years have been so crazy, with multiple house moves, failed businesses and serious identity crises, that the idea of expanding the family had pretty much disappeared.

The melody, right next to Chana's prayer, brought it all back.

And then, I had a big question to deal with: "God, why didn't you answer my prayer, the way you answered Chana? What was - is - lacking in me, that I can't seem to get my prayers to work?"

I'd love to tell you that it's just the prayer for kids that apparently hasn't been fulfilled, but the last couple of years, I've had more prayers than I can count come back with a 'rejected' stamp.

Like the prayer I should be able to find a community to belong to; or the prayer that I should be able to buy a house in Jerusalem; or even the prayer that me and my husband should finally get some peace of mind.

My rabbi teaches that no prayer ever goes to waste, so I know all these prayers are going somewhere, and doing something. But at Shiloh, I wanted to know *what.*

I can't say I got a direct answer, but I definitely got a response.

After a couple of minutes, it's like some big internal block dissolved, and God started whispering at me: "It's all good. You'll soon see why it's had to be this way. Trust me, it's all good."

And I believed it.

I left Shiloh feeling happier and calmer than I have done for at least 12 years, which is saying something.

Chana was 130 when God finally answered her prayers, and I have a way to go before I've reached that milestone. One thing I learned all over again at Shiloh is that patience is definitely a virtue. The game isn't over yet, and my prayers are still being processed - and yours are, too.

Pesach is over - I need a holiday!

So, it's a whole two days after Pesach, and I feel like....I seriously need a holiday. I'm exhausted!

Three weeks' ago, I was cleaning my house like an OCD lunatic; two weeks ago, I got some nasty virus thing that had me coughing my guts up all night for a few days; just over one week ago, I was cooking up a storm and preparing for Seder night.

Then, last week, the week of Pesach itself, I was running around Israel like a crazed tour guide, schlepping my kids here and there so they'd feel like their Pesach break was *'shavey'* (Hebrew for 'worth it').

Pesach ended motzae Shabbat, and I tried to cram two weeks' worth of 'real life' stuff into the next two days, to try and get myself at least half back on track, plus turn my kitchen back over to normal use, so I could unpack the three boxes of *chametz* I'd stuffed under my daughter's bed.

Sometimes, I ponder the Jewish holidays and I wonder what's really meant to be going on with them all.

I *have* had years where I felt more spiritually-uplifted, particularly around Sukkot time, but Pesach routinely bombs for me, spiritual-uplift-wise, every single year.

It's just so busy and frantic and stressful. How am I meant to find my soul in all that craziness?

That said, I did have a few illuminating moments, but it's really like panning for gold: I get one teeny-tiny, spiritual sliver in a whole slew of mud and mess.

Maybe I'm missing something, I don't know.

Maybe, it's just a whole big lesson in 'stop trying to control the world, because you can't.' Maybe that's why it sometimes chafes so much.

In the meantime, I seriously need a holiday...

A sense of balance

So we're in the week of Tiferet in the Counting of the Omer, which is variously translated as 'splendour', 'truth' and most notably for today's post, 'balance'.

Whatever day we're up to in the Omer, the essence of that day always translates into your actual life. Little wonder, then, that I started the first day of the week of 'balance' by having an absolutely ginormous, massive fit about the complete lack of balance going on all over the place.

I have many virtues, but 'balance' is definitely not one of them.

If I'm working, either it's full-on, obsessive crazy deadlines, projects and ambitions. Or I don't work. Full stop.

With the food, either it's green smoothies, sprouted spelt bread and gluten-free cookies. Or it's bourekas and pizza.

Ditto, with spiritual stuff. Either I'm talking to God for hours a day, working on plans to eradicate all my terrible character traits within a week, and trying to implement yet more stupid *chumrot* (stringencies). Or I can barely find the energy to do even basic stuff like wash my hands in the morning and bake challahs.

You see what I'm saying?

No balance. None. Nada.

(If my husband was reading this, he'd say that the 'no balance' thing is also an extreme. Of course I have *some* balance *some* of the time. He keeps insisting that the trait of moderation is actually there, albeit tucked far, far away, so either he knows me much better than I know myself, or he's wrong...)

This is the first year it's actually struck me how much work I need to do in the area of *Tiferet*, because usually I like to translate that as 'truth' - which makes it sound like I can take it easy - as opposed to 'balance', which is arguably one of my biggest challenges in life.

So what was today's unbalanced melt-down fit about?

It's like this: I have barely worked in any real way for 8 years. One of the big reasons I quit working is because I couldn't 'switch off' work while I was at home, which meant that I was an absent parent and wife, even when I was physically 'there' in the flesh.

A few months ago, God showed me very clearly that I can't just sit on my couch being spiritual anymore, and that I actually need to get out there and do stuff again.

With my usual lack of balance, I threw myself into the task 100% - I wrote two books in two months; I started up another website; I started planning all the courses I wanted to teach, and all the classes I wanted to give.

Wonderful!

Except, I was so busy doing all this stuff, I haven't been cooking properly, cleaning much or taking care of things on the domestic front again.

I thought I was getting away with making pasta for supper five times a week, until yesterday I realized that me and my family are starting to fall apart from the quiet neglect.

We're all exhausted from eating bad food; my house is a mess; and I'm operating in 'stuff the rainforest' mode again and made everyone eat off plastic so I don't have to wash-up. I'm so preoccupied at the moment that I'm asking my kids the same question five times in a row, because I'm not paying attention to their answers.

In short: it's a domestic train wreck.

I realized something has to change, to bring back more (dare I say it) *balance*. But here's the problem: I have no idea how to do it!

When I have projects to do, or deadlines to meet, I just kind of fall into whatever it is I'm working on, and I don't even notice no-one ate supper yet and it's approaching 9.30pm.

As always, the answer is to talk to God about it, and ask Him to help me out, here. If He wants me to be working again, in whatever way that means, then I REALLY need some help to balance that with being a mother and wife.

I couldn't find the right balance in the UK, when I had a cleaner, two dishwashers and the ability to eat out whenever I had no time or energy to cook. How I'm meant to do it now, I have no idea.

But hopefully, God does, and this is the week He's finally going to clue me in, as well.

Unclogging the pipes

One of my 'big things' is that I'm always trying to find the messages God hides away in the various circumstances of my life. Nine times out of 10, I do a pretty good job of working it out, but there's the odd occasion when I simply have no idea what's going on, or why.

Usually, they are things that are just so bizarre that they defy classification, like the time I dropped my husband off at the curb one morning and he completely disappeared into thin air.

Turns out, the council had removed that section of pavement, and my husband fell straight into a drain pipe. Thank God, he wasn't seriously hurt, but I was perplexed for weeks about what was going on, until I read something in a book talking about how using the internet was like walking on a street with massive holes all over the place.

So with that intro, let me tell you a story. This week, the washing machine and shower started backing up in my rented apartment. The landlord came, apparently fixed the problem, and left.

The next day, the toilet started backing up. I ignored it for a couple of days and hoped it was going to sort itself out, but then the downstairs neighbour told us the external outlet pipe was leaking sewage onto the street, and we needed to get it looked at pronto.

Okayyyyy, then.

All this was going on Friday morning. The plumber showed up Friday afternoon, and as soon as he started loosening the cap on the outflow pipe, it exploded. A geyser of sewage started spewing all over the pavement, and nearly knocked some passing bloke off his bike.

I looked at the plumber's face, and I could already tell this wasn't going to be an ordinary pipe-cleaning experience.

10 seconds later, a posse of 20 local neighbourhood kids showed up, and started asking my husband what was going on. He didn't have the Hebrew to go into details, but he told them 'it's *biyuv*' (Hebrew for sewage) - and they should stay far away.

Of course, they didn't.

Instead, they started analysing the contents of the disgusting mess spewing all over the pavement, excitedly announcing to everyone 'it's a number 2!!!'

At that point, I scarpered off to the local corner shop, leaving my husband and the plumber to deal with it.

I came back to find a small committee gathered around, holding a loud discussion about the state of our pipes and giving us lots of advice about how we could get someone else to pay for the plumber.

The plumber wanted to know if these 20+ children belonged to us, and whether we could get them to go away. Of course, we couldn't.

In the meantime, the stuff was still spewing all over the place, and the whole outside reeked. The audience started running around holding their noses and making loud pretend gagging noises.

I'll spare you the rest of the details by saying that we somehow managed to track down a hose, and then spent the next hour trying to clean up the mess, while the peanut gallery of eight year olds helpfully pointed out the bits we'd missed, reminding us that it was 'really dangerous'.

Two and a half long hours later, I finally slumped down on the couch, and started wondering 'what the heck was all that about?'

Sure, toilets get blocked from time to time - and it happens to us more than to a lot of people - but the sewage geyser plus audience was a completely new twist.

What was the message God was trying to send me, by spraying all that stuff all over the neighbourhood in such a public way?

My husband, ever the optimist, reminded me that it all happened on the day of '*Yesod she beGevurah*' of counting the Omer, or the 'foundation of strength'.

He's convinced that some big, fundamental spiritual pipe just got unblocked and fixed for us, based on the plumber's observation that 'that stuff's been backing up for ages. Maybe even for years.'

We only moved in a few months' ago, which means that we may well have got stuck cleaning up someone else's old fundamental issue, which just got ignored until it literally exploded in our faces (does that sound familiar?)

So what do I think about all this? Truthfully, I don't know. In the meantime, I'm just hoping the neighbour who nearly got knocked off his bike by a foul torrent of ancient cacky doesn't develop PTSD and try to sue me...

Acceptance

The last little while, I've been hearing lots of stories from lots of people with a common theme: people are being tested to cracking point in a particular area (or more usually, five areas at once); they pray, they up their mitzvah ante, they sincerely try to do everything everyone tells them to get their miracle, or salvation - and it doesn't come.

Often, not only does the miraculous salvation not show up after all that spiritual effort, the problem can even get worse.

I've experienced this myself, and to say it can cause enormous challenges to your faith is probably the understatement of the century. Thankfully, our true holy people are aware of this phenomenon, and they aren't scared to address it.

On Shabbat, my rabbi gave a shiur talking about precisely this, where you pray and pray for the miracle to show up already, and still you're stuck with the problem. So then, what does he suggest you do?

Simple: instead of praying for the problem to disappear, start praying instead to be happy with the problem.

Why? Again, simple: in our generation, we all have no end of trials and tribulations and soul corrections to get through, to clean off our 5,000 year-old slate. I've said it before, and I've said it again, that we've all been here tens of times before - and stuffed it up repeatedly - and now, there's no more second chances and we HAVE to get it right.

That's means an awful lot of soul corrections to get through, in a very short amount of time. That means, practically, that you ping from one painful problem to another, and sometimes it seems like the suffering and hardship is never going to end.

Yes, of course we deserve it! We coasted the last 50 lifetimes, we ate pork chops and lobsters, we sacrificed our children to Moloch, we chose to leave Yiddishkeit to become 'enlightened' wannabe *goyim* 150 years ago - and know we have to clean all that stuff off our souls.

God sent us down here with a lot of work to do, and so much of it is painfully excruciating and confusing and difficult. And here's the kicker: WE HAVE NO CHOICE.

We have to go through it in order to get cleaned up.

That's why sometimes, our prayers for instant salvation and mercy appear to go unanswered. If God would let up on us before we fix whatever is broken, spiritually, then what would we really accomplish?

So then, another question often starts to blossom in our minds: why bother praying, if it's not going to change anything? Great question! Here's what I think: The point of our prayers is to build a relationship with God and to ask Him to help us accept all the craziness going on in lives, not to get God to do what we want.

This distinction is crucial.

Acceptance is key; knowing that God is doing everything for our good is crucial; saying 'thank you' is the key to getting through it as fast and painlessly as possible.

So if you're going through tough times (and let's face it, who isn't?), remember the following things:

1. We're all here to fix our souls, and that requires an awful lot of work

2. Regularly talking to God will help you hold on and survive when you're reaching your fifth cracking point today

3. Saying 'thank you' is a shortcut to achieving the emuna you need to make it through in one piece

4. Accepting God's will is what it's all about.

God isn't punishing us, although I know it can sometimes feel like that. He's fixing us fundamentally, He's doing it fast, and He wants us to know one thing: He loves us, and the more we try to focus on that and accept the temporary pain when He sends it, the faster we'll get back to the good times.

Out of the box

A little while back, my oldest daughter decided to get what's called a 'rasta'. As you might have guessed, it's the usual sort of dumb teenage idea about taking a bit of your hair, wrapping all this coloured cotton. etc. around it; tying a bell on the end, and then keeping it in your hair forever (until you get sick of it and have to cut it out.)

It was that or the second earring, so I said: "OK! I let the dumb rasta!"

I realised that she'd been through a lot recently, and needed some form of self-expression that wasn't exactly *traif*, but wasn't also exactly kosher.

She got the rasta, it actually so wasn't a big deal, and that was that. She felt much happier and self-expressed and independent, and I felt like I'd got off lightly, after seeing the boy with huge holes in his earlobes where his ears used to be.

Last week, the whole family went shopping to a super-frum supermarket, to buy stuff to do a BBQ on Israel Independence Day, or *Yom HaAtzmaut*, when my kids are off school.

Independence Day is a political hot-potato in Israel, and people can make all sorts of assumptions about you based on:

» How many Israeli flags you have decorating your house and car, and how prominently they're displayed

» Whether you listen to music conspicuously on that day (as it's always in the middle of the Omer, when you're not meant to be listening to music, unless you consider Independence Day to be a quasi-religious 'holiday' like Purim)

» Whether you're buying any of the following things: BBQs, charcoal, chicken wings and skewers.

In some neighbourhoods, do any of the above and they'll stone you. In others, don't do any of the above, and they'll stone you.

We went shopping for our BBQ stuff in the big chareidi supermarket in a super-glatt part of town, where black is always the new black. We go there every week, but this week, my oldest daughter started to feel very flustered, and wanted to leave after five minutes.

"What's the matter?" I asked her.

"Ima, people are staring at me, and it's making me feel really weird."

Hmm. Why were they staring? Was it the BBQ briquettes, sticking out of the trolley? Or maybe, it was the bumper pack of hotdogs that was practically playing 'HaTikva' all by itself?

Then it hit me: it was the dumb rasta.

People's eyes were literally sticking out of their head, even though I've seen much less modest things going on with a few of the secular customers that also shop there.

Bizarre.

In the car home, my daughter explained the problem:

"Ima, you look like you're normal *dati* (religious); Abba looks like he's chareidi (black and white with payot) and I look *dati leumi* (national religious, I guess what you'd call 'modern orthodox' outside of Israel). People can't work out how we all fit together, and that's why they were staring so much."

I actually found this pretty amusing. What, does everyone dress the same in these people's families? (Ok, scratch that, it was rhetorical.)

I guess the real question I want to ask is *why* does everyone dress the same, in these people's families?

How can you have honest self-expression, acceptance and individuality, if everyone's wearing the same style? I know in my family, I have fiercely resisted 'the uniform' - but I certainly wasn't going to impose my preferences on my husband, who loves his black and white to bits.

Ditto for my kids: the rasta is dumb and borderline untznius. BUT - my daughter needs to learn that for herself, so she can get it out of her system and hopefully grow up to love turtlenecks.

After our discussion, I wondered what would have happened, if I'd gone against the clues God was sending us in the summer, and shoved our daughters into chareidi schools against their will.

One probably would have towed the line (I think...) But the other would have kicked so hard I may have lost her, at least temporarily, God forbid. But then I wonder: don't all teenagers need to be able to 'self-express', at least occasionally, however dumb and borderline tasteless it is? And if they can't do that when they're 14 without being stared at and judged, then when can they?

This year's bracelet

A few years' back, I discovered that it's a big mitzvah for husbands to buy their wives jewellery before a major Jewish holiday like Rosh Hashanah, Pesach or Shavuot. I'm very *machmir* (stringent about keeping mitzvahs), so I told my husband to release his chequebook: it was time to go shopping.

As with most mitzvahs, it wasn't so plain-sailing, at least at the beginning.

My husband came home with one duffo piece of jewellery after another, like earrings that were way too big; a bracelet that literally drew blood; another bracelet that was very pretty, but looked like it was made of plastic beads (he's still insisting they're glass...)

And so on and so forth.

Last year, I decided I had enough of all the jewellery that wasn't really 'me', and I decided I was going to pick my own stuff, and then just ask my husband to buy it. I picked a simple but very lovely bracelet and wore it happily for many months.

But then I realised something profound: each time my husband picked the jewellery for me, God used it to give me a clear message about where I was really holding in life.

The time I got the bracelet that was so sharp it drew blood, I was in a hyper-critical, judgemental mode of my life where 'cutting remarks' and 'piercing comments' were the order of the day.

The time I got the glass beads (that look like plastic) I was seriously conflicted about whether I should stay 'real' at all times, and thus be a lonely outcast, or whether it was OK, at least occasionally, to go into superficial, 'plastic' mode, so I'd still have someone (anyone...) to talk to.

The plastic beads showed up, and it took me a week or two, but then I got the message.

When I picked my own bracelet, it was gorgeous - but it was just jewellery. It didn't have any deeper meaning attached.

So before Pesach, I told my husband he was free to buy me whatever he wanted (poor guy, talk about pressure) - so I added that I would LIKE whatever it was, and appreciate its inner dimension, even if I hated actually wearing it.

He showed up with a doozy of a bracelet.

Let's be clear that it's not my taste in about a million different ways, but because I let go of my ideas and cleared the path for God to send me what I really needed, God really responded in kind.

My husband told me the man in the shop had practically forced him to buy it (even slashing the price by 75% to fit our budget) and that the bracelet was made with opal stones.

I have a gem book which tells you all the different properties of the many different stones, and this is what it said about opals:

"Opal amplifies traits and brings characteristics to the surface for transformation. Enhancing self-worth, it helps you to understand your full potential."

This is what it said specifically about blue opals, like the ones in my bracelet: "Blue opal is an emotional soother that realigns to spiritual purpose. It resonates with the throat and can enhance communication."

As I've written about elsewhere, I'd been having throat issues for ages, and the week before Pesach I actually lost my voice for a few days, so I was thrilled to bits with my blue opals.

I put the bracelet on for Seder night, and it's barely left my wrist, since. Appearance-wise, it's so not my taste. But God clued me in to the inner dimension of my jewellery, and as a result, I think it's probably the best thing my husband ever bought me.

Going back to basics: How to be grateful

For the folks who are counting the Omer, today marks the beginning of the week of *Hod*, which is connected to acknowledging God in the world, and our own mistakes, and also to saying thank you.

I kind of half-guessed that gratitude was coming up as the big spiritual work for this week, even before I went to look up what the week of *Hod* is all about, because the last couple of days I've been feeling pretty moany and complain-y again.

So I hit the first day of *Hod*, and I wondered to myself how on earth I'm meant to be grateful when that's the last thing I'm feeling at the moment?

On the way back from buying some eggs for breakfast from the corner store, God gave me some clues:

"Rivka, do you remember that time last year when you completely ran out of money and you couldn't even afford to buy groceries?"

Uh-huh. How could I ever forget? It was one of the biggest tests of my life.

"Well, you did forget. Otherwise, you'd be feeling pretty darned happy right now that you bought those eggs without a second thought."

Hmmm. I could see where this was going.

"And Rivka; do you remember when you had a really bad pain in your leg and you were finding it hard to walk around, a few years' ago?"

Well, actually not until God mentioned it again...

"Isn't it great, that you could just walk up to the corner store, and not even give your legs a second thought? You want to go somewhere, and they take you. Isn't that amazing?"

Hmmm. Well, when you put it that way, yes it does sound pretty cool.

"Isn't it great that you're going back to a house with a husband, and your kids? And they're all amazing people. And it's a cosy house, even though you're only renting at the moment. Don't you think that's great, Rivka?"

At this point, I was climbing the stairs back to my cosy flat, with my eggs, and my healthy legs, and I got it: gratitude starts with going back to basics.

The last few days, I've been getting stuck on the fact that most of my attempts to 'do' stuff are falling pretty flat at the moment, and it's been starting to get to me quite a bit.

This morning, God reminded me that true happiness and gratitude can be found in the small print, not just the big headline-grabbing external success stories that seem to be eluding me right now.

It was a great lesson and it put me in a much better mood, so I decided to pass it on to you, dear reader, in the hope that it will hopefully also help you to tap in to the true spiritual dimension of this week of *Hod*, or gratitude.

No place, and every place

I was talking to my husband a little while back (hey, that still happens occasionally, BH) when he mentioned that he was still feeling a little 'out of place'.

I see his problem: despite his attempts to blend in by wearing black and white, my husband's payot are still less than a foot long, I won't let him grow his beard past the point where I'd have to send a search party in to find his face, and the shtreimel and stripy-dressing-gown-thingy on Shabbat definitely ain't happening.

So there he is, kind of stuck being a wannabe Chassid.

I really feel for the guy. I've also spent many a long day yearning to 'fit' a little better than I do, and hoping to find a community of like-minded individuals - and feeling kinda sorry for myself that things are the way they are.

Then one day, everything changed. I was wandering around my neighbourhood doing a bunch of errands. I started out in the Old City, then I went down to Jaffa Street to do some shopping, then a little later on I found myself walking through Meah Shearim on the way up to Geula to buy some groceries.

It suddenly struck me how at home I felt in all these places, even though they're so incredibly different from each other. If I really looked like I 'fit' into any of these places 100%, I wouldn't be able to explore anywhere else without feeling like a rank outsider.

It's like all the tourists I see by the Kotel sometimes, hiding behind their cameras and i-Phones to try to quell the obvious discomfort they're feeling about being in such unfamiliar surroundings.

The upside of belonging somewhere specific is that you, well, belong there. The downside, is that then anywhere else you go kind of feels weird. Thank God, I don't have that problem. It's precisely because I don't really belong anywhere that I feel so comfortable everywhere, from the most secular spots to downtown Meah Shearim.

I suddenly realized last week what a blessing that is.

Do you know how many cool people I'm discovering, from all sorts of background and communities? There are some truly amazing people all over the place, and if I truly 'belonged' to just one community or area, I'd never know about all the other fab stuff that's going on in other parts of the Jewish world.

That day I came home and told my husband: "It's great we're social misfits! How else could we spend one Shabbat hanging out with our friends in Caesarea, and the next one in deepest Chassidville, eating our Shabbos meal at separate tables for men and women? I love that we don't fit anywhere properly!"

And now that he's thought about it a bit (and got over the idea that the gold stripy dressing gown thingy is just not on the cards...) so does he.

More effort, or more prayer?

So, about three months ago, I wrote the draft of a book about how to talk to God and fix your mental and physical health.

I tweaked it, rewrote it, tweaked it some more, then started contacting literary agents to see if anyone might be interested in helping me get a book deal. I mean, I have a blog... I've been writing for years... How hard could it be to get published?

The answer is: pretty darned hard.

Apparently, I need 25,000 followers on Twitter and 100,000 readers (minimum...) reading my blog before anyone will touch my book with a bargepole.

The good news is: I'm 2% of the way there.

What could I do? I bit the bullet and signed up for Twitter (which I still so don't get, btw) - but I can't bring myself to do Facebook. Even the thought of befriending 4000 people online gives me heebie-jeebies.

So now, I'm back to the same question I've been wrestling with for years, already: does God want more prayer before He'll bump-up my readership, or does He want more effort?

Let's be clear that before I started my blogs and new business, I'd spent approximately the last seven years ONLY praying. I had a huge reaction to my first business going down the toilet (with very little prayer and huge amounts of effort), and I felt then like 'prayer is the only way to go'.

It worked OK until my husband quit his job to join me in that approach a couple of years' ago - and we ended up going completely bankrupt and having to sell our house just to buy groceries.

That hit me like a spiritual tsunami, and I'm still picking through the wreckage of it all. But one thing was clear to me: I'm clearly not at the level where I can just sit on my couch and still be able to buy my Cheerios.

So I definitely got that message, and I reacted by trying my best to 'do' more.

But I seem to have come full-circle now, facing that same problem that's dogged me for years. If 'all work' wasn't the way to go, and 'all prayer' apparently wasn't the way to go, what does that leave me with?

I know, you're going to say 'the balanced, middle way', but as we've already discussed, balance is SO not me. But apparently, it's going to have to be. I guess I'll have to carry on doing the odd six hour prayer session, and then carry on finding random people on Twitter to connect to.

I think.

Unless you have any better ideas?

Praying: Don't force the issue

A little while back, someone asked me what I do to get my kids to pray, if they don't feel like it. I told her straight: absolutely nothing. If my kids aren't in the mood to formally talk to the Creator of the World, that's OK: they're 11 and 14, respectively.

They get forced to pray a whole bunch of times in school, so they know how to do it. And when the time is right, I'm sure they are going to want to start praying a whole lot more than they are right now.

I mean, how much did you want to pray when you were 14? When I was 14, praying was pretty much the last thing I wanted to do, and now I talk to God every day.

Sure, I want my kids to be connected to Hashem, but forcing matters is only going to backfire.

Someone told me a few years' back about their son, who was at a very serious Torah High School, where they learned a heck of a lot of Gemara, and rigorously tested the students on what they were learning.

He came out of that school hating Torah.

How could he not? Cast your mind back to your school days: is there any subject that you enjoyed *more* after being pressured to cram for it just to score an 'A' on an exam? I don't think so.

And it's even more the case with matters of the soul, because when you force your kids to conform externally, and they go along with whatever mitzvah it is you're pushing down their throat, on some level, you just completely killed the inner dimension of that mitzvah for them.

The reason I don't force my kids to pray, is because I really WANT them to pray when they get older. Praying, talking to God, is so often pretty much the only thing that gets me through my day. It's an enormous spiritual gift, and one that I want to pass over to my kids. But not by nagging them, cajoling them, guilting them or bribing them to do it.

When they're ready, it will come.

How do I know this is going to happen? Because while I don't force my kids to pray for themselves, I still try and pray for my kids on a regular basis, whenever they seem to need it (which can be every day, sometimes.)

I've been paying into their 'spiritual bank account' for years' already, and like I explained to them, when they're ready to start banking their own prayers, they should hopefully find that they've already got a fairly large amount of spiritual credit to start off with.

It's such an upside-down world, isn't it? So many of us are trying to muddle through with precious little idea of what's really right, or not, and there's so much conflicting advice out there from 'experts' who talk a good game superficially, but actually don't help you very much.

You can't force good character traits, you can only model them yourself, and hope your kids will follow suit. So if you really want your kids to pray - take the lead, and show them how to do it.

The exile of the soul

I seem to be going through a pretty heavy time at the moment, spiritually. As mentioned previously, some years it feels like every day of the Omer is an ordeal you just have to get through, and learn the lessons from.

Some years it's more obvious, some years less so, and this year - it's completely in my face from the moment I wake up.

But God always prepares the balm before the blow, so at the same time as I'm being buffeted by severe doubts about my own efforts and capabilities, and also questioning God's willingness to help me out of the pit I've fallen into, financially and spiritually, I also heard a Torah CD by Rav Ofer Erez that put everything into much clearer focus.

Rav Ofer was talking about *galut hanefesh*, or the exile of the soul. In a nutshell, he explained that the main difficulty for our generation is that we all know what's true: we've read the books, we've heard the news reports; we've done the research on Google - but we can't actually get there.

So on the one hand, *of course* we know it's bad to smoke, and bad to eat sugar, and terrible to eat margarine, and on the other hand *mmmmm, yummy donuts...*

Ditto with childrearing. Yes, we all know it's terrible to criticise our offspring, and horrendous to feed them white pasta, and border-line neglect not to have deep conversations with them at least once a month. But then, who's got the time, energy or patience for it to be any other way, especially these days?

The same is true in every area of our lives, from our marriages, to our earning abilities (*make $100k a month, from home!*) to our relationship with God. We can see how it could look, should look, has to look - and we just can't reach it.

We don't have the strength to talk to God every day. We don't have the energy to try and hold our husbands together while we ourselves are continually falling apart. We don't have the motivation to keep hanging on for a miracle rescue, even though we really do know 100% that God can give us one in a second.

Why?

Because we're stuck in 'reality', and our current 'reality' and truth don't make good bedfellows.

Which is when you can get really broken, spiritually, unless you get clued-in about what's really going on. What's really going on is that God has set up the rules in this generation in such a way that's it impossible to win the game - unless you've got a big Tzaddik behind you.

That's the only way to do it.

Spiritually-crushed people can't just go and un-crush themselves. They need outside help just to wake up in the morning, let alone to fight off their *yetzers* and start drinking green smoothies.

So if you're caught in the gap between what you know to be true, and what you want to embody, and what is actually happening in your life, join the club. It's the exile of the soul, we're all in the same boat, and it's going to take a Tzaddik of the calibre of Rebbe Nachman or Moshe Rabbenu to spring us out of prison.

Why is God a three letter word?

The last few weeks, I've been looking for other outlets to take some articles about talking to God, and actually making God a real part of your life, instead of just a nice idea.

To say it hasn't been easy is an understatement. Usually, if people are into God, they're also not into alternative health, green lifestyles and talking to God in any informal way.

And if they're into 'spirituality', then they like the whole mindfulness and meditation thing, and they dig sprout bread and energy meridians - but the whole idea of God seems to scare them off.

Clearly, there could be some big improvements on both sides of the equation, but for now, I want to know why God is a three letter word, for so many of the people who profess to be spiritual?

Mindfulness is great, as a concept, but when it's divorced from God I can't help wondering what's the point? What are you meant to be mindful of, exactly? And how is your mindfulness meant to be building the world, or actually improving yourself?

Great, I get the rose is beautiful-amazing-wonderful. But then if I don't make the connection between the rose and God, who actually created it, then what good did my mindfulness actually do me?

I have similar issues with the idea of meditation for its own sake. I talk to God for an hour a day, and I know how valuable it is to take a time out from the rush and madness of modern life to try and just 'be' for a while.

The times when I can just be, and really just explore my thoughts and reactions in a deeper way, have given me the most invaluable insights and knowledge. But only because I was connecting my be-ing to God.

If I was just sitting there trying to connect to nothing, or to shut everything else in the world out and just concentrate completely on myself (which seems to me to be the ultimate ego-trip) - then what's the point?

What is the 'nothing' going to teach me? How is making myself the centre of the universe meant to help me develop humility and insight?

Do you see the problem?

That's not to say there isn't a lot of very good things over there in the spiritual camp. Often, spiritual people appear to be far more open-minded, tolerant, and genuinely interested in the communal good, as opposed to the more narrow congregational good. Strange to say, they're also often more directly connected to their inner dimension, and their souls - which makes the paradox all the more striking that you have so many externally soul-less people talking about God, and so many externally soul-full people completely ignoring Him.

I don't know what the answer is. Clearly, it would be great if all the spiritual seekers would stop going on about 'the universe' and connect back to their Creator; and if all the officially religious folks would lighten up a bit and start to connect more to their inner dimension.

How's that going to happen? I don't know, exactly, but I can tell you what works for me: talking to God for an hour a day. When I do that, He tells me exactly when I need to ditch the fries for the green smoothies, and He also clues me in when I need to replace the 'piousness' with something a little more challenging. Like being nice to my mother-in-law. ☺

Sarah and Avraham, circa 2015

Sarah came home to the tent one day very het up. Avraham came over to ask her what was troubling her, and Sarah let rip.

"The ladies by the well are all talking about me! They're telling me that instead of staying home and kneading dough all day, I should go and get a job as a secretary, so you can just devote yourself to learning Torah, like a real *Gadol HaDor*!"

Avraham was taken aback.

"Well, but if you do that, Sarah my love, who's going to look after young Yitzhak?"

Sarah shrugged her shoulders, and said in a hesitant voice:

"Well, I saw an ad in the local 'Frum Ima' magazine that Hagar's started up a new childcare facility. I think she's roped Yishmael into keeping the kids entertained by showing them how to catch rabbits, or something..."

Avraham shook his head solemnly.

"Sarah, my love, this doesn't sound right at all. How are we meant to pass on our holy Jewish beliefs and heritage to our son if he's off shooting pigeons with his somewhat reckless brother? (Avraham always excelled in phrasing things gently.)

"How would that benefit us? How would that build the world? No, my dear, you stay home and look after our precious son, and I'll continue to study Torah every chance I get, when I don't have to look after the estate or make small-talk with the locals."

Sarah cheered up tremendously once she heard Avraham's wise words, and disappeared off to her tent to get the next batch of dough prepared.

But the ladies of the well weren't about to give up so easily. Sarah and Avraham were so, well, *old-fashioned*, and stick in the mud. It was obvious to everyone (except them...) that if a couple were really serious about the Torah, the woman had to make sacrifices to enable her husband to learn 24/7.

They dispatched Zipporah, the group's self-styled rebbetzin, to try and persuade Sarah to come round to their more enlightened view. Zipporah knocked on the tent door, just as Sarah was plaiting her challah.

"Hmm, baking again, I see," said Zipporah, with a condescending little smile playing around her mouth.

"I love to bake!" Sarah told her, eyes shining. "It fills the whole tent with such a delicious, homey smell."

Zipporah hrrmphed to herself, then sat herself down next to Sarah's kneading bowl, and put a clammy hand on Sarah's floury one, in what she hoped was an earnest, caring way.

"Sarah, I heard that Berman's bakery up the road is looking for a new manager. You'd be perfect! No-one makes challah like you, and once you start doing your bit for the family, Avraham won't have to waste so much time dealing with the shepherds and well-diggers. You'll be able to afford to hire someone to manage the estate for you, while he sits in learns...In fact, I know just the person. My sister-in-law, Estie, would fit the bill perfectly."

Sarah's smile froze on her face.

"Zipporah, I don't want to work. I want to raise my children. I've discussed it with Avraham, and he agrees that *that* is the right thing to do. Eliezer is helping us out, in the meantime, so let Estie take the job at Bermans', and then everyone's happy."

Zipporah had had enough.

"Sarah! You are being so selfish! You're married to the *Gadol HaDor*, and it's just not right that you're not enabling him to learn Torah full time! I'm sure God would prefer for Avraham to be teaching and learning Torah, than having to haggle over the price of a sack of goats' wool!"

Sarah snapped back:

"If that's true, Zipporah, then WHY did God make it the man's responsibility to provide for his wife, and not the other way round? Avraham signed the ketuba, not me!"

Zipporah rolled her eyes skyward. Gosh, that old chestnut again. I mean, it's just a *ketuba*, for goodness' sake. No-one else took that seriously. But trust Sarah to take things at face value...

Zipporah stood up to leave.

"I see I can't change your mind," she said stiffly. "I have no idea how you expect to get a good *shidduch* for Yitzhak, with your warped beliefs that men should be off supporting their families. I expect you'll get some lay-about daughter-in-law who thinks making a pot of soup is a big achievement. And the generation will just have to be an orphaned generation, bereft of your husband's Torah, because you won't swallow your pride and your funny ideas, and start your own hair accessory business..."

Sarah nodded curtly at her guest, and escorted her out the tent entrance.

Sure, Avraham's Torah was hugely important. But if Yitzhak went off the derech, then who'd be around to learn it? Or to live it? Or to pass it on to the next generation? In her heart, Sarah knew that she'd picked the right job, whatever Zipporah and the ladies of the well might say.

 # When prayer doesn't 'work' #

Recently, I was talking to a friend of mine who's been going through a very rough patch (aren't we all these days...)

This friend has been doing everything right: they've been upping the ante with their level of mitzvah observance, they've been attending more Torah classes, they've been praying more - and their life appears to be inexorably sliding towards doom and disaster.

At least, that's how it looks to them. It looks to them like God isn't giving them anything they're asking for, and that all their prayers are being ignored. My friend wanted to know: 'What's the point of continuing to pray, if God's just ignoring me, and not giving me what I'm asking for?'

Ahhhh. That's the whole crux of the matter, isn't it? Because it brings into sharp focus the whole question of whether I'm doing whatever I'm doing for *me*, or whether I'm doing whatever I'm doing for *God*.

Ask most religiously observant people why they're doing things, and most of them will tell you it's for God - and on one level, they firmly believe it. In the meantime, God gives them spouses, health, children, food and a home, all as free gifts, but this Divine generosity can feel somehow deserved, when you're keeping Shabbat or paying your 10% to charity.

Which is why the real test is when God takes it away.

Maybe, your kid goes off the derech; or your marriage starts going down the tubes; or your finances get so tight, you have to start scaling down, and scaling back, and changing your lifestyle drastically.

At that point, it's human nature to ask: "What's going on here? Why is God punishing me? What have I done wrong?"

That last comment is the clue to the underlying mind-set, which goes something like this:

"For as long as I do what God wants, and keep His Torah, God will give me stuff. If God is not giving me stuff, or has stopped giving me stuff, I must have done something wrong."

Sometimes, that's true. If a person doesn't regularly give 10% of their income to charity, for example, they may well get hit with big financial problems. If a woman isn't going to the mikva every month, her family may well get hit with all sort of massive interpersonal relationship issues. Cause and effect is definitely permanently at play, and it's often very clear and obvious.

But not always.

Sometimes, a person can be giving 10% to charity, and even 20% to charity, and still slide into poverty. Sometimes, a person can become super-duper tznius and still experience huge issues with their spouse. Sometimes, you can pray your socks off asking for something that you're pretty sure God would want you to have, like kids, or health, or a home of your own, and still not get them.

Then what?

That's when you really get to see if you're truly doing mitzvahs for yourself, or for God. At that point where all your spiritual effort comes back with an apparent 'rejected' stamp on it, that's where you're really given the choice to serve God *lishma*, for its own sake.

Often, the test is so big you can't stand up in it, at least initially.

At least initially, you'll have a huge wobble and start questioning your belief, and your faith, and your sanity. You start agonising over questions like: "Wouldn't things be easier, if you'd gone a different route? Wouldn't it be better, if you hadn't got so 'frum'? Isn't everyone else having a much easier time of it, without bothering to pray, or to change, or to grow?

I think every sincere soul-seeker goes through this process, at least once, on their journey towards God.

The answer is of course 'no'. Whatever difficulty you have as a religious person trying to get closer to God, you'd have it as a secular person trying to please yourself - and without the comfort of believing that it was somehow all for the best.

Like I told my friend, all of us today are being sent big tests to clean the slate from all the stuff we left over from our last few hundred reincarnations. That's the real cause of so many of our problems today, although we usually have no way of knowing what we actually did back then to deserve all the stuff we're getting lobbed at us in 2015.

The test is to be poor, or sick, or unhappily married, or with tearaway kids, and to know that it's not a rejection, it's not a punishment, it's just a soul correction that has to be got through.

That's why our rabbis tells us to pray to be happy with our suffering, for as long as we have to endure it. That's why our rabbis teach that some of the things we go through were ordained from the six days of creation, and there's nothing we can to do avoid them. That's why Rebbe Nachman teaches that there is no despair in the world.

Because it's not a punishment or Divine rejection. It's an invitation to judge God favourably, and to fulfil the precept of being someone who serves Him for no (obvious) reward.

And of all the tests we have to pass, it's probably the hardest.

In search of a real connection

Seven years' ago, I went cold-turkey on my internet connection, and ousted it from my house.

I didn't regret doing that for a minute, even when it meant that I couldn't find 'easy' work from home anymore, and even when it meant I had to spend hours traipsing off to the local library to email, and not even when it meant I missed out on the latest Shwekey blockbuster video.

Until six months' ago, I thought I was permanently 'off' internet, in any real way.

But then, a few things happened, not least that me and my husband realised that if we didn't start trying to make some money pronto, our next move would be into a cardboard box...

So the internet came back. Kind of.

We got one of those 'internet stick' thingies for home that work sometimes, but not always so consistently, or fast.

It wasn't ideal, but it worked well enough.

Then, we discovered that we live literally a minute's walk away from a business 'hub' in Jerusalem, where they encourage entrepreneurs to come and make full use of their free Wi-Fi facilities.

There are more chareidi men there than in most of the local kollels - and that's a good thing. Because as me and my husband realised, these days, you apparently needs some big miracles to be able to make money and be 'off' the internet, and we just didn't seem to have that much *zchut* (spiritual merit).

But then, I've discovered a few other things about the internet:

1. It really depletes my energy, physically, and I can literally feel it sucking all my juice out when I spend too long online; and

2. When you make aliyah and move to Israel, some part of you actually needs the internet to stay connected to the person you used to be.

None of my old, old friends live in Israel. Even the old friends I have in Israel don't live anywhere close to me.

Now, I KNOW that internet connections are superficial at best, but here's the thing: so are most real-life connections, these days. I've discovered it's easier to connect via Linked In than to actually go through the excruciating torture of making small talk with people I haven't spoken to for years.

And there's something kind of comforting of having some people from my past back in my life again, even if it's just via a thumbnail picture (usually circa 10 years ago...)

I don't know what all this means. I know the internet is still evil and horrible, and the cause of so much human misery. But after seven years of doing my best to be without it, God seems to have forced me back into that online world.

And the most confusing thing about it all is that it's not 100% horrible.

The film of your life

Does it ever happen to you that you sometimes feel like you're in some sort of weird screenplay of your own life? Since I've lived in Israel, every week has been so full of unusual events that I sometimes have to pinch myself to make sure it's all really happening, and not just some quirky *film noir* I've accidentally fallen into.

I don't have anything particularly 'out there' to share with you (this week...) but it's just the small, unusual circumstances that make up my everyday life that sometimes amaze and baffle me, in equal measure.

Some examples:

≫ My youngest came home yesterday, and told me a really funny, 'hilarious' story of how her friend's house in Maaleh Zeitim (a neighbourhood on the outskirts of the Mount of Olive cemetery, very close to the Temple Mount) got firebombed, by an Arab throwing a Molotov cocktail.

≫ My neighbours just bought (and subsequently sold...) a dog that was half Rottweiler, and half Pekinese. Now, I know these things are technically possible, but when I saw that super-aggressive fuzzy slipper with sausage legs, I thought someone was playing a bad joke. I mean, it kind of boggles the mind.

≫ I went out for a walk on *Yom Yerushalayim* ('Jerusalem Day') a little while back, and the streets were awash with literally hundreds of thousands of Jewish teenagers, waving Israeli flags and buying every piece of junk food in sight. It was awesome to behold, in every sense of the word.

And then there's the more routine, but no less amazing things, like the fact that I live 15 minutes' walk away from where King David is buried. Sometimes, I say a few Psalms, and then I get completely weirded-out by the fact that the person who wrote them is interred so close to my home. I mean, that's just an amazing thing.

Then, there's the soundtrack that God chooses to accompany my own particular film.

Sometimes, I'll walk into a shop and they'll be blasting out one of my favourite secular songs from twenty years' ago, and it always stops me dead in my tracks. Music comes from a very 'high' place, spiritually, and it can literally transport you across years and countries and mind-sets.

I walk into the shop a 40-something Jewish housewife in Israel, and I walk out a teenage girl in London (or Canada. The moving-around thing's been happening for decades already.)

A few days' ago, I was having a bad day and feeling completely inadequate again as a wife, mother, woman, friend and Jew. One of my kids started playing some obscure CD by Israeli Singer Gad Elbaz that we've had forever, but one of the songs, a musical rendition of Psalm 23, suddenly really grabbed my attention.

You know the one:

God is my shepherd
I shall not lack.
He lays me down in lush meadows,
He leads me by tranquil waters.
He restores my soul.
He leads me on paths of righteousness, for the sake of His Name.
Even though I walk in the valley overshadowed by death,
I will not fear evil, because You are with me.

To say I was transfixed was an understatement.

Once my kids went to school, I had the song on 'repeat' for two hours solid.

How did God know that I so needed to hear that song, just then?

How did King David know that I'd be feeling exactly that way, when he wrote that Psalm? (Maybe he also had teenage girls in his household?).

Point is, it was the perfect soundtrack for that particular scene.

I'm at that stage in the script of my life where enough suspense has built up over the last year that it's time for the denouement, already. I have no idea how the happy ending comes, but I'd like to believe it IS coming, and probably in a hugely unexpected way, like all the best plots.

Moshiach shows up on a donkey and gives my kids a lift to their school in the Old City? I find that $3 million in cash is stuffed in the pipe that keeps backing-up into my toilet? Someone gives me a fat advance to write my life story? Who knows?

All I can tell you, is that the screenplay has never had a dull moment, and while there have definitely been a lot of tear-jerking parts to it, it's been more of a comedy than a tragedy. And long may that continue.

In the mix

Musrara, the Jerusalem neighbourhood where I live, is probably the most schizophrenic place in Jerusalem. Whenever I step out of my front door, I never know what's waiting for me.

Sometimes, it's a bunch of little 'Nachmans' accidentally setting fire to the recycling bins when they get a bit too excited about burning their chametz before Pesach. Other times, it'll be a bunch of Sephardi *'arsim'* (a Hebrew slang for weird young men who have funny haircuts, a big fake diamond stud in one ear, and more often than not, an even bigger black kippa on their head), smoking a few packs of cigarettes and whooping it up around the football pitch.

Still other times, it'll be women in shawls and thick tights, or men with long payot and black hats who are studiously guarding their eyes.

And then there's the art students, who take the craziness of Musrara right up to a whole other level.

Recently, Musrara's art school decided to have an art festival for three days. Even by local standards, there were some pretty weird things going on. One art student decided to knit herself a very short dress, wear it, and then unravel the end of it and tie herself to a metal railing sticking out of the wall on one of the local streets.

She just stood there, unravelled, for hours.

Then, there were the couple on either side of the park who each had one yellow hand. They were both waving their one yellow hand around 'artistically' and singing opera arias.

It's only when we came across the 'pair' that I realised that the first woman with the yellow hand we'd seen wasn't a deranged lunatic who'd found herself hanging out at the art festival by accident.

One of the exhibits that I kind of liked was this huge tub of 'slime' (the same stuff they sell to kids in little tubs of bright green and blue, so they can indulge in all their 'booger' practical jokes) - except this slime was coloured shiny gold.

It was odd, but kind of cool to see a bunch of trendy grown-ups lining up to stick their hands in the shiny goo. The pavement was glittering like the proverbial streets of America for days afterwards.

I didn't really make an effort to participate in the festival, but every time I popped out to buy a pint of milk or pick up a bag of carrots, I found myself in the middle of it all, as it spread out into every nook and cranny.

And the weird thing was, no-one batted an eyelid that in the middle of all the 'art' and nonsense that is usually the exclusive domain of high-brow secular people in Tel Aviv, a bunch of people with long payot, or long skirts, were weaving their way in and out, trying to get on with their life.

I'm so used to the bizarre mix that is Musrara, that I kind of take it for granted now.

But after the art festival, I suddenly realized what a very special place I live in. My neighbourhood is full of people who are *mamash* 'weird' by most people's definition of that word, and also 'weird' in such different and usually opposing ways, yet we all just get on fine together.

No-one stoned or heckled the 'unravelling' lady who barely had any clothes on underneath her loose-knit dress; no-one started up with any of the juvenile Nachman's, who kept trying to fiddle with a couple of the more interesting exhibits, like the remote-controlled 'bongo playing' machine set up on the basketball court.

Dare I say it, there was a lot of peace and love going on.

It's easy to preach tolerance and acceptance when you exclusively talk to, and surround yourself with, people who look and think and speak exactly the same way you do.

In Musrara, no-one talks tolerance (at least, not in my circles) - but every day, we live it. And it's beautiful.

Third time lucky with Perek Shira

Around Purim time, a good friend of mine suggested that I should start saying Perek Shira for 40 days for my husband. After our 'Meaning of Life' tourist attraction in the Old City sank without a trace at the end of 2014, taking a large chunk of our house money with it, my husband got pretty down about the whole thing, and was finding it hard to pick himself up again, and make a plan for the future.

I sent him to Uman, I did a *pidyon nefesh* for him - all things that usually work, and how. But this time, I wasn't seeing so much improvement.

But when my friend suggested doing Perek Shira, I pulled a face.

The first time I signed up to do 40 days of Perek Shira, around nine years' ago, I did it in the merit of my finances turning around, and that I'd be able to pay off all my debts and buy a home again. On day 39, we got an email from the people buying our house telling us they were invoking the 'forgotten' clause in the contract, and kicking us out six months earlier than planned.

Uhh, God? How was *that* an answer to my prayers?

I'm still not entirely sure, but our finances kind of did look up again for a couple of years', and we did pay off our huge debts and buy another house again (at that time).

But all this took a good couple of years' to materialise.

The second time I did Perek Shira was again for our finances, this time around two years' ago. Within a few weeks of completing the 40 days, my husband decided he couldn't stand being a lawyer any more and we got plunged into a period of extreme financial turmoil that led to (yet another...) forced sale of our house, just so that we could afford to buy groceries.

Long story short, it seemed to me that Perek Shira was having the *opposite* effect of whatever it was I was praying for, so I wasn't very keen to try it another time, even though I've heard so many miracle stories of how it's helped other people.

But my friend wouldn't take 'no' for an answer - their 30-something sister got unexpectedly engaged the day after someone said 40 days of Perek Shira for her - and so I found myself stuck saying it again.

This time, I kept it really simple: I wasn't praying for specifics like money or a house. I just prayed that my husband should rediscover his *joie de vivre* and come back to himself.

The last few months had taken us both so low, that even that required a supernatural miracle, at that point in our lives.

But the third time is the charm. From day 1 of saying Perek Shira, I noticed my husband was changing. Slowly, slowly, he was regaining his self-confidence and optimism, and ability to try things again.

He decided to go back to being a lawyer and he sorted himself out a couple of pretty snazzy websites, literally in a couple of days. He found a great place to work. He started to have ideas, and plans again.

By the end of the 40 days, he'd made the first real money for our family in two years. We were still a little stuck in the tunnel, but the end had been sighted, and a big, fat light was now shining out of it.

Amazing!

There's an idea that you have to publicise the miracles you get, with Perek Shira (and probably with every miraculous salvation God sends you.) I didn't really have what to say the last two times, so I couldn't.

But it's really been third time lucky with Perek Shira. It brought my husband back to himself, it gave us both renewed hope that we weren't going to end up living in a dumpster, and it turned round a period of such intense emotional anguish and despair that even hours of personal prayer and repeated visits to Uman were barely making a dint in. (Apparently.... these things are never how they seem.)

So give it a go, and try Perek Shira for yourself. God is listening. He does care. It's just sometimes, for whatever reason, there can be a huge time-delay on our prayers getting answered. The trick is to not give up while you're waiting for an answer, because sooner or later, it WILL come, and life WILL get sweeter again.

Feeding the gorillas

Last week, my husband decided he needed to get a phone that would let him send texts (but nothing else...) which sparked off a frantic round of 'musical mobile phones' in my family.

When the music stopped, I'd ended up with my daughter's old phone, she got my husband's old phone, and everyone was happy. Then that particular daughter started popping off to her room for some 'quiet' time with alarming regularity.

I thought to myself: 'Maybe she's stressing out about the end of year play....Maybe she's overwhelmed by all the bat mitzvah prep...Maybe one of her teachers is giving her a hard time...' Then one morning, I went to wake her up - and she was already awake, playing on her new phone.

The penny dropped.

Turns out, there's some really cool zoo game on my husband's old (apparently not as kosher as it looked) phone, where you have to keep feeding the animals every day, or they die.

My kid was hooked on feeding the electronic gorillas.

Now, I've learned enough to know:

1. Confiscating the phone is only going to backfire
2. God is using the gorillas to show *me* something about me and my life
3. I HATE how slimy modern technology actually is.

I explained to my daughter that she was addicted to her phone, and she agreed.

"But if I don't feed the gorillas, they're going to die!" she told me plaintively.

In the meantime, she'd been so caught up in feeding the gorillas she'd forgotten to feed her real life hamster for a week, and it was looking a little peaky, to put it mildly.

But I digress.

I left my daughter, and made my way back to the laptop, that's been consuming a bit too much of my life this past week. As I plugged in the internet stick for the 4th time that day, my husband raised a quizzical eyebrow at me (I had huge internet addictions 8 years' ago, and that's one of the reasons I got it out of the house.)

"I have to check my emails," I explained plaintively.

Then it hit me: I sounded just like my daughter, caught up in the fantasy land of feeding pretend gorillas.

Maybe the excuse was a bit more convincing, but I could see it was exactly the same stupid principle at play: If I don't check my emails every few hours, all my online opportunities and connections are going to die....

But really? They're not. And if that does actually happen, then they were probably as genuinely useful and real as my daughter's gorillas.

Standing up for God

Someone told me that the United States has just legalized gay marriage across the whole country. That same someone (who lives in the USA) told me that she had a feeling she'd be moving to Israel sooner rather than later (even though she hasn't been here for years) because "Once you start messing around with the seven Noachide Laws, that has a way of diminishing God's love for your country."

I know reams and reams has been written about this landmark decision of the US Supreme Court. I'm not going to add to all the speculation and punditry, but what I DO want to talk about is how important it is at this stage in Jewish history for us Jews to stand up for God.

When I moved to Israel 10 years' ago, it was a little ahead of the first 'gay parade' in Jerusalem. Back then, I was still working for the British Government as a ghostwriter for Ministers, and one of my best clients (in terms of how much work they asked me to do for them) was the Women and Equality Unit.

But in terms of what I had to write for them, it was the most drecky, horrible job ever.

In just one speech, I'd have to laud women who rushed back to work as soon as their kids were born (the 'women' bit); praise Muslims for having six wives (the 'equality' bit), and then also toss in at least one comment about how great and wonderful same gender relationships were (more of the 'equality' bit).

And bizarrely, in that ultra politically-correct environment where any notion of 'right and wrong' had gone completely out of the window, no-one seemed to notice how all these ideologies were completely at odds with each other, out there in the real world.

I hated those speeches.

I hated the feeling that I was selling-out my soul and my beliefs just to pay my mortgage - but of course, that's exactly what I was doing because back then, the Women and Equality Unit paid me very nicely to turn those things around for them.

It was part of the equation of being a religious Jew in *galut*, or exile.

So we moved to Israel, and all the fuss about the gay parade broke out here, and I kind of watched it from the sidelines, a bit bemused. My Israeli rabbis were encouraging me to take a stand, and to sign petitions against it, and to register my displeasure. And part of me really wanted to do that stuff - but the other part of me was far too scared of doing anything so un-politically correct, because, well, political correctness was a central plank of my career and bank balance.

Or so I thought at the time.

So I felt very uncomfortable, but I did and said nothing.

Fast forward a decade, and a lot of water has flown under the bridge since then. I learned a lot more about some of the deeper reasons for God's commandments, and I also gave up my career, and went through a patch of 'being' instead of doing that lasted for quite a few years.

In that time of enforced career failure, my ego took quite a beating and I started to realize more and more that God is running the show.

God is putting food on my table (or not...) God is paying my bills (or not...) God is responsible for my successes in life (I'm ready when You're ready, Hashem).

That understanding helped me to start shifting all the political correct brainwashing out of my system, and to stop worrying that if I stood up for what was right, in whichever way God expected that of me, that I was going to lose my cred, career or bank balance. I anyway lost all of those things, which was a very painful process, but now I see it has a huge upside:

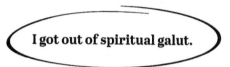

I got out of spiritual galut.

I can say GAY MARRIAGE IS REALLY BAD, and not care about the consequences of making that statement.

But if I was back in the UK? Or still working for the Women and Equality Unit? Now, you're talking about a huge moral test - and the chances are high that I would probably fail it.

The decision by the US Supreme Court to legalize gay marriage is both a huge test, and a huge opportunity for God-fearing Jews. Anyone who can stand up for God is effectively proving they're out of slavery, out of exile, out of bondage to foreign beliefs and political correctness. Anyone who can't (and man, believe me that I know that there's bills to pay and tuition to cover) - is stuck, spiritually, in a very bad place.

A place where God is missing, and man's desires and animal-self is ruling the roost.

So the choice is simple, but also incredibly profound: Stand up for God in whichever way you can.

Or stay in spiritual exile.

Beautiful lies, vs. ugly truths

At the moment, I'm starting off most of my daily chats to God with a frank admission that I'm not doing so well, spiritually. The events of the last year proved to me once and for all that I'm really not the Tzaddik I thought I maybe could be, and that I'm actually in a much lower place than I thought.

For example, I thought I was really past reading secular information. I don't use the internet! I only read Jewish books! I am completely free of foreign ideas and knowledge!

But these days, I'm reading a whole bunch of books on holistic healing methods, and I just took the horrible step of starting a Facebook page to help me publicise my new book, when it comes out in a few more weeks, God willing.

Did I sell out?

I don't know. All I can tell you is that after spending two years on the breadline, and having to sell my house just to cover my basic living expenses, I realized I'm not on the level where I can happily live in a dumpster.

I've tried everything I can to avoid being on the internet, but God seems to have dragged me back to it.

Let's take another example, namely all my efforts to see God behind all the 'difficult' people in my life. Sometimes I manage it OK, other times their horrible, hypocritical behaviour has me seething and frothing at the mouth again.

Now, I KNOW God is behind it all, and that if I have emuna I should believe that God is all there is, and that He's doing everything for my eternal good.

But whenever I get another 'holier-than-thou' email from a very troubled person who has no idea how nasty and messed-up they really are, I often still react very negatively.

It usually takes me at least a couple of days of doing some serious talking to God about it all to remember that:

a. God is behind it all

b. It's all for my best

c. Hoping that these people get run over by a bus is NOT the optimal spiritual response that God wants me to have.

But sometimes I wonder: does my reaction to the crazies mean I have no emuna?

Emuna means bringing things back to God, and while I can't always get there immediately, that's usually the place I end up after I've chewed it all over for a while.

So I do have emuna, at least eventually, but I've also realised that I'm not a big Tzaddik who can continue to turn the other cheek as people keep slapping it. (Whoa, now that I've written that I'm seeing that probably, 'turning the other cheek' to lunatics is not even an authentic Jewish idea. Wrong religion, mate...)

I could tell you another million other things that I'm struggling with at the moment, but it all comes down to this:

God prefers our ugly truths to our beautiful lies.

Yes, I could lie through my teeth and tell God how much I love covering my hair, and going to the mikva every month, and avoiding movies - but He knows that right now, the only reason I'm doing a lot of my mitzvahs is just because God wants me to. I'm not getting a huge amount of *nachas*, or personal enjoyment, out of quite a few things at the moment.

Does the fact that I'm doing a bunch of mitzvahs *lishma*, i.e., only for God, make me less holy, or even more 'religious'?

I don't know.

The only one who really knows is God, and as long as I continue to keep it real, and to keep bringing everything back to Him, I know that somehow or other, God is satisfied with me, however lowly and imperfect I really am.

Everything you do is meaningful

It's a very comforting thought to believe that even just trying to do something is enough to potentially tip the world closer towards God and good, even if no-one ever knows about it.

The outcome isn't what makes all the things I'm trying to do meaningful. It's meaningful just because I'm putting my effort into it, and I'm trying to do what God wants.

And the same applies to all your stuff, too.

Like that blog you started doing last year, but gave up on because 'only' three people were reading it. If you enjoyed doing it, if it was meaningful to you, carry on doing it! Don't give up! Every word you write could really be changing the spiritual dimensions of the world for the good.

Or, like those songs you started working on, but never quite got around to doing anything with. Take the plunge and book some studio time! Who cares if it's not so professional, or if the quality isn't as good as the Rolling Stones? As a believing Jew, everything you do in the world is meaningful.

And this also applies to the smaller things that none of us get any kudos or Nobel prizes for, like making our kids supper, and cleaning our toilets, or biting our tongues when we really want to let some jerk have it.

It all comes back to the idea of *ratzon,* or free will. Ratzon is really where it's all at.

What we WANT makes all the spiritual difference in the world, regardless of the outcome. Why? Because while the *ratzon* is down to us, the outcome is 100% up to Hashem.

If you internalise this idea, it can change your life. It can inject meaning into even the most mundane, mind-numbing chore in the world. It can encourage you to keep writing, keep teaching, keep singing, keep learning, keep sharing, keep inspiring, keep loving - even when there doesn't seem to be a whole lot of kudos coming back from it all.

Keep going dear reader, because every single thing you do is meaningful, spiritually, and it really could be bringing Moshiach and *geula* a huge step closer.

And that applies even if no-one else knows about it, even if no-one else applauds it, and even if your Google Analytic stats still completely suck.

The challenge of staying tznius online

I hit a huge problem when I came back online after a seven year hiatus from the 'real world'. (You know, that place where appearances count for almost everything, and where you have to be very careful to play the game, if you want others to take you and your ideas seriously.)

The online world is a pretty untznius, or immodest, place to be if we define tznius in terms of trying to avoid attracting attention. On the one hand, pretty much the only point of doing anything online is to attract attention. On the other hand, attracting attention is the classic definition of 'untznius behaviour'.

So I've been sticking my toe into these murky waters very cautiously indeed, to try and feel out the least immodest ways of participating in the fundamentally immodest process of getting noticed on the web.

Man, it's so hard! A little while back, I hit my first real big bump on the road to getting noticed as a writer, when one of the sites I'd contacted to see if I could write for them turned round and asked me for a full frontal picture, to accompany my pieces.

10 years' ago when I lived and worked in the UK, this wouldn't even have crossed my radar as a potential spiritual problem. When you're regularly shaking hands with a load of Toms, Dicks and Harrys every single day, posting your picture online is just not an issue in the same way.

But now? Now, I'd spent seven years living in Israel and trying to refine my behaviour. Now, I didn't shake hands with strange men, and I did my best to avoid getting into unnecessary conversations with the opposite sex. I came *off* Facebook almost a decade ago, for Heaven's sake!

So now, being asked for a full face photo was actually a big deal. I ummed, I ahhed, I tried to find a way around it, like obscuring most of my face behind a huge gerbera - and the editor who asked me for the picture was seriously unimpressed.

That opportunity vanished into thin air.

I've been continuing to fudge the issue with my woman-cum-gerbera picture for a few months' now, until God sent me a brainwave to get a cartoon picture done. It's still a fudge, I know. It's still not really 'tznius', I know, (what is, on the internet?), but given my impossible requirement to attract as much attention as possible in the most tznius way, it ticks a lot of boxes.

Another area where I'm struggling, modestly-speaking, is being in contact with members of the opposite sex. For the last few years', I've been out of the workforce, and I could pick and choose who I was interacting with. Online, I can't.

I'm still trying, in whatever small way, to keep any necessary emails with men I'm not related to short and to-the-point, but I know I'm fluffing it up sometimes. I know it's not ideal. I know that God is not schlepping nachas from me 'linking in' to a bunch of strange blokes.

But I don't really know what to do about it all.

And then, there's the *coup de grace* of untznius online behaviour, and that's Facebook.

Ah, Facebook.

How I hate it. How I've done my best to avoid it all costs over the last 10 years, and how distressing I'm finding it to have to bow to the inevitable, and sign up for a new account.

Facebook for me is purely business. I'm not 'friending' anyone I already know, I'm not spending any time ogling other people's cute kids pictures. I'm just making the bare minimum effort I need to make to *get noticed* online, to give my book a chance of selling.

But my heart still sinks every time I have to log-on to try and promote my Facebook page. I don't know what's more depressing: that so many people are wasting so much of their time and energy generally commenting and liking and posting, or that so few people are currently doing that on my page.

The thought that I'm actively encouraging more people to waste more of their life in my direction is profoundly disturbing.

But I don't know what to do about it all.

I spent years asking God to show me a more modest way of getting my stuff noticed, without really getting anywhere.

In the meantime, I'm consoling myself with the thought that there really is no perfection in the world until Moshiach comes. When he shows up, even the internet will have to clean up its act, and it will be possible once again to sell books about talking to God even if you don't do Twitter or Facebook.

The King David cure-all

Last week, after months of running around like a crazy lunatic trying to pull off 5,000 things at once, I completely burned-out.

I could feel it coming for a few days, but I had a bat mitzvah to celebrate, and a big list of things on my 'to do' list, so I hoped that if I got an early night or two, that would be enough to turn it around.

So I carried on for a couple more days until one morning I woke up so mentally exhausted I almost couldn't move. I couldn't cook. I couldn't shop. Nothing. All I could do was sit on a couch and read a bit, and even the reading was pretty taxing.

Uhoh.

That state of utter exhaustion has happened to me before, and in the past it's taken weeks and even months to really recover from it.

This time, I realized that if I didn't slam on all the brakes ASAP, I was staring another bout of chronic, long-term exhaustion in the face. So I told my husband: "I can't cook! I can't schlep another kid to another bat mitzvah party! I can barely move! I just have to sit still, and recuperate."

God helped me out by arranging for the gas company to remove my gas meter (by mistake, apparently) so my oven wasn't working anyway.

Ironically, I didn't even have enough energy to do my usual energy exercises, or to make my usual healthy smoothies, so on the day I crashed, I just ate a big bar of chocolate for lunch.

Uhoh again.

Before I went to sleep, I dabbed a load of aromatherapy on my pyjamas and I stuck a bunch of strength-inducing seeds on my hands, and I had a very early night.

The next day I felt a bit better for the first half an hour, but then I started to feel incredibly weak again, like I was going to fall over. I took it really easy and ate a lot of salad, which helped a bit. But by evening, I was still feeling pretty rotten.

Physically, I was actually OK, but mentally I was completely wasted and beyond burned-out.

I was just starting to worry that I was going to be out of action for weeks or even months again, when God sent me a brain-wave to nip off to the tomb of King David, and spend a bit of time there.

One of the amazing things about where I currently live is that King David's tomb is a 20 minute walk away. My husband came with me, and I took lots of breaks on the way to sit down and gather my strength for the next 5 minute walk - and finally, I got there.

I sat down - and it hit me like a wave how spiritually depleted I felt. Like I was completely washed out, and washed up. I sat there for 20 minutes, and what can I tell you?

I came out feeling a whole lot better.

I walked home with no rest-stops; I had another early night; and the next day, I woke up feeling almost back to normal.

With all my healthy eating, and energy exercising, and med-itating, God reminded me yet again that maintaining a strong connection to our Tzaddikim, both alive and dead, is what's re-ally keeping me going.

We live in very tiring times. I've lost track of the number of people who've told me recently that they feel like time is speeding up. The truth is, that it is, and that the modern world is a very exhausting place to be.

So if you're also cracking under the strain, clear your desk, cancel all appointments, order in pizza for supper and head off to King David, (or your nearest big Tzaddik) for an immediate pick-me-up.

It's cheaper than a spa (unless you have to fly in from somewhere), it's faster than a face-life, and from personal experience, I can tell you that it really will rejewvenate you.

What's with the socks?

So there I was, minding my own business in the start-up hub right next to my house, where I go to do all things internet-related, when this super-stressed businessman suddenly showed up, and started politely demanding that I give him my seat.

He had a big Skype call to make in a minute...blah blah blah.

He just HAD to sit in the place I was sitting...blah blah blah.

If was the only place with a neutral backdrop for his call...blah blah blah.

I could move back there when he was done...blah blah blah.

In his polite, bullying way he managed to strong-arm me out of my chair, while he then went on to make one of the most tedious, long-winded and loud Skype calls in the history of mankind (when I left 3 hours later, he was still going.)

I have to say, the whole incident left me fuming.

The more time elapsed, the angrier I got at him. I mean, who did he think he was? Why was his Skype call automatically more important than me, and what I was working on? Why didn't I stand up to him, and tell him to get stuffed (in a polite, British way, natch)?

That last question really held the key to it all, as when I went to talk to God about it the next day, I could see that the bullying businessman had managed to press on some very old buttons about being able to stand up for myself, and defend myself.

Until I started talking to God about what had just happened, I'd forgotten that I was routinely bullied in school for years. When I was asking God to show me *why* this whole incident seemed to have gotten under my skin in such an extreme way, He brought up a memory from my second day of high school.

My old non-Jewish high school in the UK was the epitome of goyish snobbery: it had a swimming pool; it had its own coat of arms; it was 450 years' old and it had such a strict uniform that even your underwear had to conform to the rules, or else you were asking for big trouble.

I didn't know it at the time, but I can't stand uniforms. The one caveat in the school uniform code was that for some strange reason, you could wear white or red socks, as red was the official school colour and therefore, blessed and holy.

I only had two pairs of official school socks (white and red, as per the uniform list). I wore the white pair the first day, and the second day, I showed up to school with the red pair, completely oblivious to the fact that you didn't actually *do* those kind of things.

That lunchtime, I was sitting on a bench by the playing field, minding my own business, when a gang of second year girls suddenly showed up out of nowhere, and started picking on me.

"Don't you know that only cheap women wear red?" one of them asked me (I was 11 and she was 12. It just goes to show you the moral level of non-Jewish society 30 years' ago in London, doesn't it.)

I wasn't entirely clear what she was talking about, but I knew one thing for sure: I was being bullied.

I ran away crying, and that was the first and last time I wore those red socks to school.

Now, as the grown up me, I know that God is in the world, and that God arranged the whole thing.

But I think it was only this morning that I started to get a glimmer of an idea why those girls gave me such a rough ride about my socks. Red attracts a lot of attention, clearly bad attention. Even though I was completely naïve and clueless, God was ensuring that I wasn't going to be wearing those red socks again - and it was an act of love, albeit I didn't realize that at the time. Anything but.

Strangely, as soon as I went back to the socks episode in school, my huge animosity towards the bullying businessman also kind of disappeared. I think God just sent him so that I'd go and rescue that 11 year old self from thinking God was 'bad' because He sent me a bunch of bullies on the second day of my new school.

Now I can see that the guy has huge issues, and is a *nebuch* (sad case). If he asks me to move again, I'll appreciate I'm dealing with someone who could probably use the number of a really good shrink, and I'll move happily because, hey, thank God I'm not him.

For a few hours there, I was questioning God's goodness again, and wondering why he had to send me another bully, at the age of 41. After talking to God about it all, nearly all my issues have dissolved, and I have a lot more clarity and peace of mind.

But if I hadn't taken that spiritual time-out? I had at least 10 different strategies planned out in my head for how to let the bullying businessman have it, next time round.

That guy has no idea what a debt of eternal gratitude he owes to Rebbe Nachman.

HOW TO JUDGE OTHERS FAVOURABLY EVEN IF THEY'RE REALLY ANNOYING

» Remember they all had very difficult childhoods (even if it doesn't look that way) and grew up feeling unloved, worthless and despised, in some way.

» Remind yourself that God is just using them as messengers.

» Understand that what's really irritating you about them is something that's really irritating you about yourself.

» Remember that if you get more of the 'bad' out of yourself, you'll be able to handle them better.

» Don't make their problem your problem

» Minimise the time you spend around them

» Do lots and lots and lots of talking to God about it all, to work out what's really going on, and what's the spiritually correct way of responding

» Understand that their ability to change is very, very small (It's like when God hardened Pharoah's heart - some people have picked 'bad' so many times, they really can't get access to 'good' anymore.)

» Remind yourself that it's just a test or spiritual *tikkun*.

(And this last one is really the best piece of advice for dealing with the crazies...) Remember that YOU might actually be the crazy one, here.

No more blame game

Until recently, I used to have an automatic tendency to try to blame other people for causing my problems.

At work, it was my demented colleague who was causing me all the issues.

At home, it was my kids who were messing up my house and wrecking all my plans.

It was always *other people's fault* that I was angry, or stressed, or rushed, or upset.

I was thinking about how much I used to play the blame game this morning, when I accidentally smashed my last treasured glass from a long-ago Italian holiday, because one of my kids left it in the sink under some other things without telling me.

As I shifted the plates out the way to start washing up, I heard the sound of breaking glass and sure enough, my last pretty yellow goblet from Venice was history.

You know me well enough by now to not be so shocked when I tell you that for the first five seconds, I still got pretty upset, angry and blaming.

"*WHO* left the cup in the sink!?" I started shouting at the top of my lungs.

But then, I remembered that God is running the world, and I calmed right back down again.

It's currently the three weeks, a time in Jewish history known for trouble and calamity, so if God was fixing it that I was probably getting a small difficulty via a broken glass, I was getting off pretty lightly.

Sure, it had sentimental value. Every time I saw it, I used to think of that Venetian holiday we took before my kids were born...and then I'd start feeling a bit weird that I couldn't afford to do that in a million years' now, even if I wanted to...and then I'd remember how much spare cash, and what a nicely done-up house I lived in then...and to cut a long story short, you can see how God actually did me a favour by smashing that cup.

When you really try to see God behind all the stuff in your life, even the annoying, upsetting, frustrating things that your kids and husband do, life really does get a ton more sweeter and easier to manage.

But it's not a fast process to see the world through those non-blaming eyes, and it takes years and years of reminding yourself, and training yourself, to actively choose *against* the blame game, and to see God.

To give another example, just now as I sat down to type this, I leaned back in my desk chair and nearly fell off it backwards, twingeing my back in the process. The same annoying kid who was behind the cup getting smashed (albeit, indirectly) had been fiddling with the levers on my chair (it's summer and she's bored...), transforming it from a cosy office chair to a dangerous, life-threatening contraption.

Again, for the first five seconds after that happened I was livid. I've spoken to her on a number of occasions about not touching the chair, and this time I really hurt myself. I saw red for a few seconds...until I remembered that God is running the world.

God arranged for me to hurt my back by falling off my chair.

I still asked my daughter to leave my chair alone (for the millionth time) and explained what had happened, but I did it in a much calmer tone, without trying to load a ton of blame, guilt and shame on her for trying to cripple her poor mother.

Afterwards, I marvelled at myself: How did I manage to do that?

The answer came in a flash: only with a huge amount of Heavenly Help, because believe me, it was an open miracle.

My daughter is definitely benefitting from me trying to opt out of the blame game, but truly, the biggest winner is me. When you play the blame game, even if it's convincing, it still leaves you with a ton of anger, resentment, vengeance and hatred to have to work through and dispose of.

That stuff puts such a huge load on your nervous system, and directly impacts your emotional and physical health, albeit in ways that are often very hidden.

The less I play the blame game, the lighter and happier I feel about things. Even when my family heirlooms get smashed; even when my back gets thrown out; even when people do or say some very hurtful things, because knowing that God's really behind it all makes is so much easier to come through smiling.

Turning anger into compassion

One of the things that Jews regularly ask God is that He should 'transform His anger into compassion'.

I've been thinking about this idea a lot recently, because my husband told me an idea he read in Likutey Moharan that explains that God often takes His cues from us.

For example, if someone is working very hard on transforming their own feelings of anger into compassion, God is much more likely to take that person's prayers on the subject of turning His own Divine anger into Divine compassion much more seriously.

I guess you could sum it up by saying God hates hypocrites. If we want Him to act nicely with us, and to overlook all our many millions of shortcomings and issues, He wants to see if we're willing to act like that with other people.

Now, here's the thing: it is SUCH hard work to regularly turn your anger into compassion (or at least, it is for me.)

Not a day goes by where I don't read something, hear something or experience something that triggers off some massive rage fit. All this anger, and judgement and self-righteous disgust bubbles up - and dear reader, it always feels so just and proper at the time, especially when I've just discovered some particularly nauseating behaviour - and then I have to work like a dog to try and calm it all down again.

Depending on the circumstances, one session of talking to God about what's going on is often enough to dissolve the problem, or at least, my negative and angry reaction to it.

But sometimes, I find myself working on the same old problems, the same old difficult people, for days, weeks and even months at a time.

Just when I think I've *finally* put my angry feelings to bed about a particular person, they'll go and do something even more annoying or disgustingly hypocritical, and then I find it all bubbles up again.

My *yetzer* starts whispering at me that it can't be right to just keep letting these people off the hook, and to keep judging them favourably. Can't I see how horrible they are and what terrible things they're doing and causing?

Literally, I can go round that mental track for a whole hour, noticing all the bad, disgusting stuff about a whole bunch of individuals, and then trying to figure out how to judge it all favourably, and bring it all back to God.

Let's be clear here that BAD ACTIONS are always bad, and must be clearly recognised and responded to as such. But BAD PEOPLE is a whole different matter. Just because someone killed a granny in cold blood (BAD ACTION) doesn't mean they themselves are completely evil and bad (BAD PERSON).

See, I told you it's really, really hard to pull this stuff off.

But I'm still trying, not least because I know that there is no such thing as human objectivity. Every single one of us is adept at judging our fellow's behaviour in very stark, harsh terms, while making a whole pile of good excuses for ourselves about how we just HAD to kill that Granny, because really she was the secret head of Hamas, or something.

To put it simply: I want God to tie Himself in knots to judge *me* favourably, and to turn whatever anger He might have against *me* to compassion, so I have to practice what I preach.

But it's so hard, and sometimes I get despairing and give up.

To keep me going, God has taken to sending me more, and more profound insights into human behaviour, so that I can really start to understand a little more why people do the things they do.

For example, I recently really got, for the first time ever, that certain people are so fundamentally obsessed with self-preservation that it literally blinds them to any other consideration.

Their *yetzer* tells them that 'X needs to happen at all costs, in order for you to feel good and happy and safe', and then off they go, dead set on making 'X' happen regardless of who they have to squash or crush in the process.

Now, I'm not excusing the BAD ACTIONS, but I'm starting to understand that BAD PEOPLE are incredibly messed up, vulnerable and generally pathetic human beings. The more I'm seeing that, the easier it's getting for me to switch out of anger and into compassion mode.

At least, sometimes.

The whole world is about to flip right side up...

So, other people's dreams are always really boring, I know, but bear with me because I had a 'repeated' dream yesterday that I want to share with you.

The Gemara tells us that all dreams are generally considered to be nonsense, but if you get a dream which is repeated, those ones you should take a little more seriously.

So here goes:

The first time round, I was walking somewhere with huge pubs that were covered in shiny gold writing = clearly London.

I got to a massive football stadium, like Wembley Arena or something, and I could see that the arena was up in the air on top of the world's biggest rollercoaster, and that any minute now it was going to loop-the-loop and completely flip over, like rollercoasters so often do.

My kids were with me, so I made sure we were sitting down and properly buckled in, because when you don't secure yourself properly when you're on a rollercoaster, you can end up getting smashed to bits on the floor, when they start flipping over.

But me and my kids were pretty much the only ones wearing seatbelts! Everyone else was just sitting there, completely unaware that they were actually on a huge rollercoaster half a mile up in the sky, and not just having a picnic or something.

I couldn't get why they didn't know what was about to happen, and why they weren't buckling up. Just then, JFK showed up and started shooting people (clearly, the 'pure nonsense' part of the dream) and I woke up. It was 2am.

I fell back asleep - and the dream happened again, except this time my kids weren't with me, and the stadium-cum-rollercoaster was packed with even more people. This time around, most people had a vague idea they were on a rollercoaster that was about to flip them completely over, but they weren't dealing with that idea in any sort of rational way.

Some people told me they were just going to 'hold on to the grass' where they were sitting, to stop themselves from falling. Others showed me how they were going to use all their strength to somehow 'dig in' to the earth, and that was going to be enough to keep them on board. And still others disappeared into the toilets for a smoke, just as the 'fasten your seatbelts sign' flashed up.

I woke up again, and I immediately thought of the story in the Gemara where two holy sages are sailing around on a boat, when they stop on what they think is an island.

They make a fire and start cooking their supper, when suddenly the whole 'island' starts shuddering, and completely flips over, because really they were camping out on the stomach of a huge fish.

The sages testified that if their boat hadn't been so close by so they could easily scramble back into it, they would have both drowned.

It's a parable, of course, and at least one of the commentaries I've seen on that particular Gemara equates the boat with Moshiach, and *emunat Tzaddikim*, or belief in our holy sages.

One thing's for sure: whenever the world really does flip over, you REALLY need to make sure you're buckled in, and hanging on to something solid. And if my repeat dream is anything to go by, the rollercoaster ride that's leading to geula could really be starting soon...

The showdown

We're not going to get geula with big speeches, or by sending out big, preachy emails to four million people telling them to dress more tznius ASAP, or else.

We going to get redeemed when we treat other people with more love and consideration, and when we recognise the profound truth that there is one thing 'wrong' with the world, currently, and that's us, ourselves.

God showed me that very clearly a couple of days' ago, when I ended up having a show-down on holiday with one of my teenagers.

In fairness to her, she really didn't want to come on holiday with us in the first place, and I persuaded her to. Also, our car's air-conditioning was broken, because we drive an old banger that's nearly as old as our aliyah, and we moved to Israel 10 years' ago. Also, we were going camping, which meant there was no air-conditioning when we reached our destination, either. Also, she spent three hours tucked under a huge quilt, because there was no room for it in the trunk.

And lastly, we tried a shortcut through Nazareth that ended up adding an hour to our trip in the middle of a sweltering hot July heat wave day.

So we got to the camping ground, and the next thing I know is that my daughter's in 'short t-shirt' sleeves and has hitched her skirt to above-knee level, to go and paddle in the stream running through the campground.

I went ballistic.

I mean, I'm a *FRUM* Jew, and frum Jews don't do things like remove layers of clothes just because they're about to pass out from heat exhaustion...

Long story short, we got into a huge row, and all these horrible words and thoughts started to bubble up in my head, and some of them even escaped out into the open.

I felt terrible. My daughter felt terrible. My husband and other kid felt terrible.

My husband suggested that we go into town, and find somewhere with air-conditioning to calm down a bit, and eat something. My daughter refused to come. While my husband was trying to change her mind, I felt another bitter volcano of angry resentment well up and rushed off to the car, before I made a bad situation even worse.

While there, I asked God for some serious help. "God, I'm treating my daughter horribly. Please help me! Help me to see past the short sleeves, and reach out to her!" Because you know what, I used to wear far less clothes than that at her age, and she's basically a really good kid, and not some evil baddy out to destroy all the *kedusha,* or holiness, in my home.

Suddenly, my anger started to evaporate, and I really, really just wanted to be back on the same page as my kid, even if that meant letting go of my pious standards and expectations.

My husband watched me rush out of the car, and got a bit worried I was about to do something rash. Who knows, maybe I did.

I apologised to my still hurt and misunderstood kid. I told her I wanted her to come with us, even with her short sleeves, because SHE was what was important here, and I loved her and accepted her regardless.

She could come with short sleeves, and with her above-the-knee skirt, and I'd try very hard to ignore them. I'd also buy her whatever (tznius) clothes she wanted in bulk quantities, if she'd let us patch things up, and just come.

So she came.

And after I spent 500 Nis (around $150) buying her some really nice stuff that was still a serious bargain, I then spent the rest of the afternoon pondering what God really wants.

For sure, God wants my daughter to dress modestly. For sure, He also wants me to have a good relationship with her, and to keep seeing the good and treating her compassionately, too.

I put myself in her shoes for a few minutes, and I could see that at that age, I probably would have reacted exactly the same way, if not even worse.

And now look at me ;-)

Point is, God has a lot of patience for our young people, and a lot of love for them. And as Rav Natan of Breslov wrote, when something is true, it brings you closer to God, and it doesn't push you further away.

Continuing to make a point about her sleeves would have only pushed my daughter away, long-term. Maybe I would win the tznius battle (and that's a big maybe), but for sure, I'd lose the tznius war.

She'd be another kid that when she got a bit older, she'd ditch the skirts completely in favour of jeans, as soon as she could actually do what *she* wanted to do. I don't want that. I want her to serve God happily from her own free choice, which means I need to give her some space now.

Afterwards, my husband told me that he thought my making peace with my daughter had done more to bring *geula* forward than anything else I'm up to at the moment.

If the reward is commensurate with the effort and the difficulty, then I think he might be right.

Who's in control, here?

In some ways, I'm very lucky: my oldest daughter has been in difficult 'teenager' mode since the day she was born, so I'm actually used to being challenged, argued with, and forced to look at the side of myself that I'd rather just ignore.

The whole thing with teenagers, and with kids generally, is that they are just coming to teach us something about ourselves. The sooner we work that out, the easier they are to deal with.

Their obvious 'bad' is just my secret 'bad', and once I realise that, (and I get over my urge to run away from my family), some sort of solution to the problem usually starts to present itself.

So like I was saying, this particular kid is extremely strong-willed, and extremely difficult to control in any way, shape or form (as well as being very sweet, and a genuinely good, kind, loving person.) Now, I also have those tendencies, but I've always seen them as positive: I'm very principled, determined and hard to corrupt. It's quite a shocker to realise that maybe, at least occasionally, I might also be quite annoying and even (gasp!) plain wrong about things.

Anyway, my daughter is a huge *neshama*, and I know for sure she's going to set the world alight at some point, hopefully in a good way. But in the meantime, I'm having one 'control' argument with her after another, and it's driving me bonkers.

Let's be clear that I really do know that I'm not in control of anything, and that God is running the world. At the same time, I keep coming up against my daughter's *yetzer hara*, that's insisting on keeping her out with friends until all hours; insisting on going to Netanya for Shabbat to spend time with people I've never even spoken to, let alone met or know anything about; insisting that she doesn't want to come on holiday with us, or insisting that limiting her phone time to *only* 18 hours a day is completely unreasonable.

On the one hand, I'm trying to nullify my ego and control-freak nature as much as possible, and on the other, she's only 14 and is occasionally plain wrong about things.

But it's taking me hours of prayer to work out if I'm arguing 'my side' of things for her, or for me. If it's ultimately for her - then I can stick to my guns and know it's OK. If it's for me - then I know it's not going to end well, and I'm risking alienating her, God forbid.

It's such a narrow bridge, and I frequently have no idea of where it's actually taking me.

At its root, I'm struggling with two main issues:

1. It's sometimes so hard for me to keep seeing the abundant good in my teenager, and to not believe the *yetzer*'s propaganda that she's just doing things to be awkward or rebellious.

2. I'm sometimes still forgetting that neither she, nor I, are really in control. God's running the show, God's setting up all the tests, God's making me stubborn like a mule, and making her stubborn like a mule.

One of us has to break the deadlock by acting like a grown-up, and as I'm 41, that job seems to be falling to me.

But it's so flipping hard! It's so hard to let go of some of my deepest-held principles in order to send my daughter the clear message that SHE is what's important here.

More important than what I want; more important than keeping her elbows covered in 40 degree heat; more important than my daydreams of what she should be, and say, and look like and believe.

I want her to be able to serve God as her, which means letting her discover who 'her' really is.

I was hoping that 'her' would like to plait her hair back, wear blue shirts and black loafers, and be enamoured with davening.

But just like that could never work for me, that's not working for her, either. She has wild hair, a huge personality and a penchant for wearing the biggest earrings I've ever seen in my life.

Sigh.

Until I realise, I'm not in control here, and that's the way God made her.

For His own very good reasons. For the best. Because she's got her own unique job to do in the world, and blue button-downs simply don't figure in there.

And who am I to question God?

But Shabbat in Netanya is still out of the question.

Get knitted

This year, I found the Nine Days pretty hard going and emotionally intense. To put it a different way, I was blubbing like a baby for almost a fortnight, and felt like I was getting hit with one emotional tsunami after another.

I'd have one massive 'issue', talk to God about it, try to learn the lessons or make the *teshuva* (repentance) I needed to, feel good again - and then the very next day, I'd get hit with another massive issue to work on.

By day eight of the Nine Days, I was a complete wreck, so I did what I always do in those circumstances, and sought some solace in God's company. As I live 15 minutes away from the Kotel that seemed like the natural destination to do some emergency talking to God, so I took my knitting, and went.

I took my knitting for a few reasons:

1. I'm in the middle of knitting a shawl, and it's going to take me months to finish it.

2. Knitting while I talk to God sometimes helps to keep me focussed, especially when I'm somewhere 'busy' like the Kotel, where I can get carried away with looking at everyone else instead of doing what I came to do.

I don't often knit and pray, but I'm going through a stage of doing that at the moment, and for this time and place in my life, it's working for me. So I got to the Kotel, I sat down off to the side, I took my knitting out, and I started crying my heart out as quietly and unobtrusively as possible.

I had a lot of heartache well up and break out again, and from past experience, I know the best way to deal with it is to let it surface, speak honestly to God about what's hurting me, and then wait for Him to tell me what's really going on, and why it's going to be OK.

So I talked a bit, knitted a bit, cried a bit, sat a bit, on and on, for a good hour until I finally started to feel better, and the tears were starting to dry up. I'd knitted one and a half rows, and they were pretty wonky, but inside I was starting to feel much more pulled together and OK again.

Which is when the old bag swooped in and attacked.

At first, I thought she was asking me for the time, or something, so I gave her my best friendly face and tried to pay attention to what she was saying. What she was saying, in Hebrew, was this:

"Tell me: have you asked a Rav if it's OK for you to be knitting at the Kotel?"

Once I understood her, I started to see red (I'm half Moroccan, and very occasionally, it shows.)

"Why should I ask a Rav?" I asked her. "What's wrong with knitting?"

She didn't know, but she just felt I should ask a Rav, because she was sure it was wrong (it goes without saying she was as 'frum' as they get, padded headscarf and all.)

I tried to explain that I was knitting while I was talking to God, which is when she really started having a go at me, because it was completely forbidden to talk to God while doing anything else!!!!

At this point, something snapped and my Moroccan Mrs Hyde completely took over.

"Tell me," I asked her, "have you asked a Rav it it's OK for you to be embarrassing people in public like this?"

She tried to tell me that she wasn't, and that she was only trying to give me 'rebuke', like you're meant to.

"OK," I snarled back. "Let's make a deal: I'll ask a Rav if it's OK to knit, if you ask a Rav if it's OK to treat people in such a nasty way, and to have a go at them in front of so many other people. And if you like rebuke so much, you can have as much of it from me as you want, just give me the word..."

At that point, she turned on her heel and left.

I sat there fuming for another five minutes with my knitting in my lap. What an old bag! What a hypocrite! The whole time she was berating me she'd been holding her prayer book open at her place in the middle, because she'd interrupted her own 'devotions' to come and have a go at me.

Then, I started pondering what the message was, and also, should I finish knitting my row?

After all, God was behind that old bag, and maybe He wasn't so impressed that I was knitting at the Kotel? I did some more talking to Him about it all, and here's what I got:

The lady was a test, to show me how much things had changed. In the past, I've been bullied a lot in various circumstances, and God wanted to show me that I could handle the crazies better now, and that I could stand up for myself, and that I didn't have to feel like the perpetual victim anymore.

The second thing I got is that I should knit another row, just for God. (I have to say, that bit surprised me a little.)

God helped me to see that talking to Him and working on myself, knitting or not, is the most precious way I could be spending my time.

So I carried on purling, and by the end of the row and my visit to the Kotel, I felt so much better.

Don't give up, dear reader, if you have an obstacle, or wig-wearing bulldog, trying to pull you away from your conversations with God, however modest or imperfect they appear to you.

They're changing the world, really.

I think that's why sometimes, they attract so much negative attention.

Entitlement vs gratitude

A little while ago, I got repeated phone calls from a young couple who wanted to come to us for a meal on Shabbat. We'd had them a few months' ago - it was OK, but nothing special. The conversation was pretty stilted, and my girls left the table after a few minutes, because it was *borrringggg*.

Unfortunately as the host, I couldn't join them in their room. So I soldiered on with our taciturn guests, making polite conversation until it was the bless-ed time of grace after meals.

Like I said, I've had worst shabbat experiences, but I've also definitely had better ones, and I wasn't so keen on repeating the experience any time soon. In the old days, I had a huge fear of being 'guest-less' for shabbat, but the last couple of years have been pretty solitary in many ways, and as a result I've learned to not only tolerate 'family only' shabbats, but even to welcome them.

Add into the mix the huge amounts of stress I've been under, in various ways, over the past few months, and *voila*, we reach a situation where I often don't have shabbat guests, and I've got a lot fussier about who sits by my table.

(I know: what can I tell you? I'm definitely not Artscroll Biography material.)

So when this young couple asked if they could come again, I told my husband to make our excuses and decline. Behind the scenes, I was having quite an intense 'teenager' time, and I also didn't have a lot of spare energy and *koach* for guests. It was that time a couple of months' ago when even cooking for *myself* had become a bit tricky.

A few weeks' on, the couple asked again. Again, we made our excuses. My kids had friends staying over, and from our previous experience with them, this couple didn't really 'combine' well with anyone else.

A few weeks' on, they asked again. Again, I had far too much going on in my life to handle guests, and I told my husband to decline. Which is when I started to ponder to myself: what's going on here?

I mean, if I'd told them the first time to come whenever they wanted, and to just call me whenever they felt like it, and that it would be a pleasure to have them - that would be one thing and I'd have no complaints.

But I didn't, and I hadn't, and to keep calling after repeatedly being told 'no' set some alarm bells ringing.

Even in university when I was dead skint and had one armchair that I'd rescued from next to the dumpster, I used to invite my friends for meals and Shabbat suppers. Even when I was a young, newly-married, 20-something (and still dead skint...) I used to have guests almost every week.

It's just something me and my husband did, and it never depended on us having a lot of cash or a perfect home.

By contrast, something that me and my husband never, ever, did was invite ourselves over to someone else for shabbat - barring the one time I asked really good friends if we could come for lunch last minute, as I'd been caught up in a crazy situation all day and hadn't been able to buy or cook anything myself.

With good friends, you can do those things and it's ok, because it's clear that you're not just after a free lunch, and that there's some mutual caring and reciprocity going on.

So we can argue it's just an age thing, a stage-in-life thing, but I don't think I agree. I invited people decades' older than me for meals in London, right from the first month I was married.

After pondering it, and wondering if I've just got plain mean in my old age, it struck me that's what's bothering me about all this is that there doesn't seem to be any reciprocity on the table. It feels as though there's an expectation that I'm just meant to happily have this couple for shabbat, *ad infinitum*, with no friendship, caring or concern in return, simply because I'm 41 and been married for 18 years.

Why?

Who said?

I've had times - plenty of them - when I was terribly lonely on Shabbat. I've also had times when I could barely afford to buy a chicken for Friday night supper - but I never expected someone else to fill that lack for me. That would be making *my* problem *their* problem. What I have done to alleviate my loneliness, more times than I can count, is to reach out to someone else, someone new, and to invite *them* over to *me*.

I know, what a shocking thought!

But just maybe, God is giving this young couple plenty of quiet and lonely shabbats for a reason.

Maybe, He wants them to dig a bit deeper, to see past themselves and their wants, and to start to realize that if you're the one that's offering to cook, one way or another you'll always have company around the Shabbat table.

At the crossroads

Last week, my daughter went for a BBQ with a bunch of her friends from the old neighbourhood. It was the typical 12-year-old girl affair: lots of smoke, squealing and 'fun'. But the next day, one of the girls who'd been at the BBQ collapsed unconscious and was rushed to hospital.

There, she was given drugs that set off a huge allergic reaction, completely collapsing one lung and half-collapsing the other. She was fighting for her life for a couple of days.

Meanwhile, back in my home my daughter was having panic attacks, shakes, couldn't eat, and couldn't sleep. Part of the problem is that no-one knew, initially, what had caused my daughter's friend to collapse in the first place, and the 12-year-old girl network thought it had something to do with the fumes from the fire starter spray they'd used to get the BBQ going.

My daughter had also breathed in those fumes a bit (no more than usual, though) - and was now consumed with anxiety that the same thing was going to happen to her, and that she was also going to collapse, God forbid.

After a lot of heartfelt prayers, the friend's condition stabilised after five days. It's still not great, but it's not life-threatening the way it was.

The whole episode did my head in, because it underlined with a big, black pen the complete fragility of life. One day you can be barbequing with your friends and whooping it up, and the very next day you can be fighting for your life in intensive care.

Without God, and emuna, in the picture you'd go completely bonkers.

At the same time that all this was going on, someone sent me a very poisonous email that completely floored me.

When you write publicly in any capacity, poisonous emails are unfortunately par for the course, even when you're writing for the 'frum' Jewish world that's apparently meant to know better.

That poisonous email showed up when my emotional coping abilities weren't their best, and it pulled the tiny bit of the rug away that hadn't already disappeared as a result of what was going on with my daughter's friend.

For a few days afterwards, I went into a massive slump and started questioning the point of continuing to write on Emunaroma, and opening myself up to personal attacks from very disturbed individuals.

If I've learnt one thing, it's not to make decisions when I'm reacting to circumstances. So I spent a few days' praying about it all and asking myself some tough questions, like: Maybe, writing about my own challenges isn't so *tznius*? Maybe, the things I'm sharing here aren't so useful or helpful? Maybe, there are better things I could be doing with my time and my keyboard?

The answers are still a little fuzzy.

What I do know is this: I'm at a crossroads in my writing, and in my life at the moment. Today marks 10 years of being in Eretz Yisrael, and I feel like something is about to shift in the direction my life has been going in, hopefully in a very positive way.

I don't yet know what it means for me, and for Emunaroma. Part of me believes that if I'm still getting poisonous emails from people who really should know better, I should just give up already, and go do something safer and more enjoyable.

The other part of me believes that if I'm still getting poisonous emails from people who really should know better, I'm probably on the right track, spiritually, and I shouldn't be deterred.

Trouble is, I don't know which part is right.

The most crucial parenting skill of all

If someone asked you 'what single thing is going the make the biggest difference to your child's emotional health,' what would you say?

One person might say that the most important thing would be to teach them how to be a mensch. Someone else would maybe put the emphasis on self-discipline, and that their kid should know how to get places on time and tie their shoelaces the right way. Yet another person might say that the single most important thing should be that their child feels loved, 'seen' and respected (OK, that's three things, but you get the idea.)

Me?

I think that the one thing that makes the single biggest difference to a child's emotional health is how much humility their parents have. Let me explain what I mean.

When you've been working on your character traits for a while, and trying to get your ego reduced down as much as possible, that's when you can actually start to internalise the idea that despite your best efforts, you're not a perfect, infallible human being, and you never will be.

Let's be clear that reaching this level takes a huge amount of spiritual striving and effort, and it doesn't happen overnight. But once you start to even just approach this level of genuine humility, it completely changes how your view yourself and your interactions with other people, and particularly, how you view your relationship with your children.

With that introduction, here's my top five reasons why humility is the most crucial parenting skill of all.

A HUMBLE PARENT:

1) Doesn't automatically assume that they're always right. This cannot be stated too strongly. Sometimes, even the best-intentioned, most well-meaning, genuinely empathetic parent in the world can still be plain wrong about things. They can still make mistakes - sometimes, even huge mistakes - in how they relate to their children. They can still cause damage, pain and suffering to their children, even when it's genuinely the last thing they'd ever want to do.

It takes humility to admit that to yourself.

It also takes a lot of humility to admit that to your children, and to openly acknowledge that you probably messed up a whole bunch of times, at their expense.

The good news is that just the simple act of admitting we aren't perfect *too our children* goes a really long way to fixing the damage.

2) Can 'hear' what their child is actually telling them.

One of the hardest things to deal with in an emotionally-healthy way is when your kid decides to travel a path that suits them, and who God designed them to be, but which goes against your dearest held principles or ambitions for them. When the first earring in the nose shows up, or the first tattoo, or they tell you that they want to drop out of medical school to go and be a gardener, or musician, or something, it can cut a parent to the quick. The more humility a parent has, the more respect they'll accord to their children, and the better they'll manage to react when their child chooses something that is not in alignment with the parent's own wishes and desires.

3) Doesn't make their own problem their kid's problem.

The more humility you have, the less you try to pin the blame for your own character faults and issues on other people. If you're yelling at your kids, it's not because 'they're acting too wild', or 'winding you up on purpose' (even if they really are...), or because they're 'acting disrespectful', or to 'teach them a lesson'. We yell at our kids because we have anger issues. Full stop.

We all have a whole bunch of negative emotions and issues that we all need to identify, acknowledge and accept, and our kids excel at helping us to uncover them.

Kids are just our mirrors. If we fix the issue in us, we'll fix it in them, too.

4) Understands that parenting is giving, not taking.

Writing in 'Education with Love', Rabbi Shalom Arush explains that parenting is giving. We give to our children all the time - and yes, sometimes it's really, really hard work. But 'giving' doesn't just means material things, like clothing allowances, luxury holidays and the latest i-Phones. Real giving includes a number of things that are sometimes much harder for us to part with. Like time, effort, sleep, comfort and always having things our own way.

Without a big dose of humility, it's impossible to really give, and to continually put what's best for your child above what's best for you.

5) Asks God for help.

Humble parents realize that even when they make their best effort, they're still going to make a whole lot of errors and mistakes with their children. They understand that they need as much help as they can get to raise happy, healthy, emotionally well-adjusted kids, and they'll go straight to The Top to get it.

It requires humility to go talk to God about your parenting, and to admit that you're not feeding your kids right, or spending enough quality time with them, or messing them up with your hypochondriac tendencies, rage fits and obsessive house-cleaning habits.

The truth?

If we could fix these problems ourselves, we would. It takes humility to admit that not only are we flawed, we can't actually do much to fix our parenting problems and our own emotional issues. But once you put God in the picture, you can relax: your bit is to act humble and ask for help. His job is to help your kids turn out just fine, regardless of everything you did or didn't do for them.

Compassion for the parent, compassion for the child

Between the ages of 27 and 35, I found it really, really hard to see my kids' point of view about anything, really. If *I* was tired, they needed to go to bed *now*, regardless of how much energy they still had. If *I* wanted to spend the day traipsing around some ancient village (which I find endlessly fascinating, but which is the epitome or borrrringgg for most people under the age of 30) then *that's* what we were going to do on our day off.

If I wanted to eat something interesting, and they didn't - they were being too fussy, and they should learn to branch out a bit, and extend their palate.

Then I hit a very tough stage in life, when God suddenly showed me that there was a small, immature part of me that had been squashed for years, and who was now causing me no end of problems as a result.

That younger me, or *inner child*, had also been routinely ignored, bossed around, emotionally crushed or neglected, and put firmly on the back-burner, and now, it was making me pay an enormous price in terms of my physical health and emotional wellbeing.

The more I listened to my 'inner child' the more I realised that all the bossing around, ignoring, shouting and neglect that my inner child had experienced had profoundly affected her (and me). It had made her scared of the world, paranoid, cynical, super-defensive, very angry and most of all, plain ill.

So for the next five years or so, between the ages of 35 and 40, I kind of switched sides, and started to find it very difficult to see the 'parents' point of view about anything, really.

Sure, sometimes we're tired, exhausted, stressed, burned-out - but that doesn't mean we can use our kids as verbal punch bags, or take out all our frustrations on them, or use them to try to patch all the huge, gaping holes we suddenly discover in our own lives and souls.

Not that parents do this on purpose, of course, because most of us don't have the first clue what we're actually doing to our children when we repeatedly put what suits *us* over what's truly best for them. I certainly didn't, and I always considered myself to be a caring, compassionate parent (broadly speaking. I'd also have massive guilt-trips when my inner child would start whispering a few home truths in my ear about how selfish, manipulative, emotionally-absent or controlling I was actually behaving around my kids, but I could usually make it shut up and go away, sooner or later.)

I kind of got stuck in that place of 'good kids' and 'evil parents' for quite a while, and it had some huge repercussions on my relationship with myself, my kids and my own parents, most of which turned out to be very healthy and positive developments, ultimately.

But a few months' back, God started to clue me in that there was a more balanced, healthier 'third way'. Developing some more compassion and getting past my own inner anger was the key to stumbling on this third way.

After spending literally hours, weeks and months asking God to help me reduce my anger, and up my compassion, one day He suddenly sent me an insight that changed the whole picture:

When grown-ups act like jerks, and treat other people horribly, it's just because really, they're still treating *themselves* like that. If they're yelling at their kid, ignoring them, abusing them, getting angry at them, hating them, even, it's just because they're doing exactly the same thing to themselves, and their own *inner child*.

I have to tell you, this revolutionised the way I started to relate to 'bad parents' and nasty people.

It's still a work in progress, but I'm starting to see a *derech* develop ahead for figuring out a system of parental education that is based on compassion for the parent, AND compassion for the child - because really, they're suffering from exactly the same problems.

It's a cast-iron spiritual rule that kids R us - whatever problems we have that we haven't resolved, worked on or acknowledged simply sprout-up in the next generation, often causing the parent no end of heartache.

That's certainly what's happened to me.

The answer is to treat the kid more compassionately - but here's the huge revelation: a parent can only really do that if they first treat THEMSELVES more compassionately. If they're beating up their kid, then they're for sure also beating up themselves, someway. If they're angry, super-critical and cold with their kid - guess what? Yup, they're doing that to themselves, too. If they're strict, unforgiving and expect perfection from their offspring, you already know who else is suffering tremendously from those exact same negative and unhealthy expectations.

It stops being about parent vs. child, or about what's good for me vs. what's good for them, and instead becomes about what's good for BOTH OF US.

And that's a completely different equation from making one party the permanent bad guys.

Uman redux

So, you remember my daughter's friend who nearly died as a result of an allergic reaction to the medication she was given, three weeks' ago? (She came out of hospital this week, BH.)

My daughter had such an extreme reaction to what had happened I decided we had to go to Uman ASAP.

Usually I try to go with a tour group where everything is taken care of and arranged for you, but this time round, I told my husband to book whatever flight he could find and arrange whatever lodging was available, to get us to Uman before school started.

We went for a 36 hour round-trip, and as with all trips to Uman, it was eventful.

Usually when I go to Uman by myself, I just sit in the Kever and do some longggg praying sessions. But this time, I had a couple of kids to think about, and when one of them showed up right at the beginning of my planned six hour prayer-a-thon, I realised God was giving me a steer to re-prioritise how I was spending my time.

Getting my priorities right, and achieving balance between 'me' and 'family' has been an ongoing struggle for me, for years already. So when I got the nudge to stop praying, and to actually spend some time with my kids in Uman, I took it as a sign.

Rebbe Uman wrote something like: 'It's a shame to be in Uman, and not visit the Sofia Park.' On most of my trips, I've shunned the outing to the Sofia Park to spend more time praying at the Kever, but this time round, we ordered the taxi, and went.

The Park is beautiful - full of the sorts of mature trees that I used to see in abundance in the UK (which is pretty much the only thing I actually still miss.) We spent a very calm, tranquil couple of hours walking around, and having the first 'lazy Sunday' type outing we'd had in a decade.

It was so nice.

But then I pondered, is *this* really what God wants me to be doing? To put all this time, money and effort into coming to Uman just to spend time wondering round a landscaped park?

The answer, perhaps surprisingly, was 'yes'.

Because even though we're souls clothed in bodies, the body still needs some time and attention, and giving it what it needs is actually an enormous mitzvah. I'm learning this lesson very slowly still, but I felt this trip to Uman underlined it for me.

Usually, I dump my bags in my room and rush straight off to the Kever. This trip, we wandered around the pizza place and corner store buying food before we even got to the apartment. Then, my kids started browsing in one of the local 24/7 trinket shops (that doubles-up as the French Crepe Café) before any of us had even got anywhere close to visiting the kever.

It was the opposite of how it usually is for me: materialism in place of spirituality; spending money on 'stuff' instead of giving it away to charity; doing the tourist thing around Sofia Park instead of doing six hours by Rebbe Nachman's grave.

But strangely, this trip to Uman started to teach me some very profound lessons about achieving balance, and noticing my family, and the importance of just being. I sat in the park, and just sat. I sat on the bench waiting for a kid to pick out a cheap 'Uman' souvenir, and I just waited. I sat by the side of the road for an hour waiting for the taxi to show up that was going to take us back to the airport, and I just looked at the sky and breathed.

I realised, I do this so little.

I'm so busy in my head, in my writing, in my 'doing', that even when I'm praying, I'm still 'doing' instead of 'being'.

In Uman, you get that flash of clarity, that lightning bolt that lights up the whole path for a moment, an hour, a day, and shows you where you could actually get to in your life. Then you get back on the plane, and it all goes dark again.

The challenge is to recreate that clarity, and to integrate it into your own, real life.

That's what I'm trying to do now, but I already know I have an uphill struggle to stop doing so much, and to start being more.

But at least now Rabbenu's shown me the way, I know it's possible.

The secret of forgiveness

Rosh Hashanah is right around the corner, and I've been thinking about:

> **Why is it so incredibly difficult to say sorry?**

Before you read on, you might want to take a minute or two and think about what's stopping you from making that much-needed apology to the person or people in your own life. When I started pondering this, the following things popped-up in my head as possible reasons why it's so hard to ask for forgiveness sometimes:

Maybe it's so hard to ask for forgiveness because it's:

» Embarrassing

» Demeaning

» Unpleasant

» Makes us feel like we want to throw up

» We actually don't feel like we did anything wrong

» We're still far too upset at the other person to say sorry

» Let THEM come to ME and say 'sorry' first!!

» Apologising is going to cause me to lose my power or influence in some way – other people won't respect me anymore

» Apologising is going to make me feel even more terrible about myself, if I actually admit to doing something wrong

» It's too painful

Anything else? Did I miss anything out?

Because now we're moving on to the next tough question I've been thinking about:

> **Why is it so hard to accept someone else's apology?**

I'm not talking about the small 'nothings' that most of us find it all too easy to forgive, like when our host 'only' putting out three salads for Shabbat lunch instead of the usual six, because she had a tough week. Or when our friend apologises because it took her a few hours longer to return our person's phone call.

I'm talking about the big stuff here.

Like, the horrible comment someone made that devastated us. Or the completely thoughtless behaviour that ruined our wedding / bris / bar mitzvah. Or, the decision or action that changed the whole course of our life, and caused us a lot of suffering and heartache.

Big stuff.

So now, that person finds out it's Elul, and that they need to make amends to the people they've hurt, and they phone you up to apologise. If you're like most people, you're not going to immediately drop your guard and gushingly accept. Sincerely accepting apologies from people who have really hurt us is actually really hard!

Why is this?

Again, each of us will have our own particular reasons, but when I was musing about why it can be so hard to accept apologies for big things, the following things came up:

» We don't trust it's a sincere apology

- » We're scared if we let our guard down, they might hurt us again
- » We want them to suffer EVEN MORE!! (i.e., vengeance)
- » We still have a lot of feelings of hatred against them (that's not politically correct to say, I know, but still true)
- » If they person who's doing the apologising has caused us a huge loss or damage, we can't forgive them because we're still blaming them for the horrible situation we still find ourselves in
- » It's not fair!! Just saying sorry after the terrible thing they did to us is NEVER going to be enough...

Anything else you want to add to this list? Because now we're going to move on to discovering that:

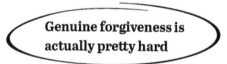

Genuine forgiveness is actually pretty hard

As you're hopefully starting to see for yourself, sincerely asking for forgiveness when you know you've done something bad, and sincerely forgiving someone else who really hurt you in some way, is actually really, really difficult to do in practise.

(SO STOP BEATING YOURSELF UP IF ALL THE FORGIVE-NESS STUFF IS NOT COMING EASY! IT TAKES 120 YEARS TO PERFECT ALL THESE NEGATIVE CHARACTER TRAITS!!!)

But Hashem still wants us to do all the 'forgiveness' stuff, and He's particularly keen that we do it in Elul, so that we go into Rosh Hashanah, the *Yom haDin*, with as clean a slate as possible.

God relates to us *midda kneged midda*, which means 'a measure for measure.'

If we forgive others, He'll forgive us. If we ask forgiveness for others, He'll forgive us. And this is a deal that has some eternal ramifications, because Gehinnom doesn't atone for sins between man and man; it only takes care of the sins we didn't make teshuva for, between man and God.

If we stole something and didn't give it back and ask the other person for forgiveness – we'll have to come back again to fix the problem.

If we hurt someone with harsh words and we didn't sincerely make amends – we'll get sent back here to sort it out, and this time it could well be that WE'LL be the ones getting the verbal abuse, as spiritual payback.

If we didn't somehow fix the fallout from that juicy piece of gossip we shared with 50 of our closest friends on Facebook, then guess what? God is going to send us back to rectify the blemish we caused to our soul.

So forgiveness, as well as being really, really hard, is also really, really crucial for our spiritual rectification process. So how exactly are we meant to do it (especially when those people who have hurt us the most are still trying to pretend that they're perfect, and didn't do anything wrong?)

Read on.

Learning how to forgive

One of the Baal Shem Tov's students once asked him the seminal question: 'Why do bad things happen to good people?' In response, the Baal Shem Tov sent him to a well in a nearby forest, and told him to go and climb up a tree close by, and watch what happened next.

The student was a little confused, but hey, it's the Baal Shem Tov! And he knew that his holy teacher certainly had good reasons for giving him these strange instructions. The student found the well, climbed the tree, and waited.

The first person who came along, stopped at the well, took a big shluck of water, then walked off – but the student saw that he'd left his fat purse of money behind him, at the well.

Next, a young lad came along, saw the purse full of money, and happily took it away with him.

A third person came along, stopped at the well for a drink – and got beaten up by the first person who'd discovered his lost purse, and had come back to claim it. When he couldn't find it, he was convinced the last person there had stolen it, and started beating him up, so that he'd confess where he'd hidden it.

When it was all over, the bemused student climbed down the tree, and came back to the BESHT for an explanation.

The Baal Shem Tov told him:

"In a previous life, the first person who lost the purse was a litigant in a trial where he should have lost and been liable to pay a lot of money – except that he bribed the judge to decide in his favour.

The second person who found the purse was the other litigant, who was dishonestly swindled out of his money. Now, the account has been settled.

And the third person who got beaten up, was the crooked judge."

The secret of forgiveness

It's a simple story, but it teaches us a profound lesson about how we can really start to forgive other people, namely that:

God did, does and will do everything in the world.

That's the first of the Rambam's 13 Principles of Faith, and it's a fundamental tenet of Judaism.

But how does knowing that God is doing everything in the world help us to ask for forgiveness, and to forgive others? Let's find out.

Let's start by seeing how this idea changes the whole picture when we need to ask for forgiveness.

A little while back, I got an email from a lady who was having some ongoing, chronic health issues that no medicine or antibiotics was resolving. My correspondent started talking to God about her health issues, and they started to improve.

A little later, she sent me a heart-wrenching email asking for advice on how she could make teshuva for messing up her grown-up kids, who were depressed, angry and struggling with their emotions and relationships.

My correspondent had had a very stormy relationship with her spouse, and there was a lot of anger, yelling and tension in the house which spilled-over into her parenting. She was blaming herself mercilessly for all her kids' problems, and didn't know what to do next.

Before I continue, you should know that the situation my correspondent described is unfolding itself in so many homes today, even the most orthodox Jewish ones. Spiritually and emotionally, Am Yisrael is in a huge mess, and my correspondent's dilemma resonates with that secret part of every mother today, who secretly fears that she's messing her kids up.

And we probably all really are!

Here's what I suggested she should try to do:

1. Apologise to the children themselves for her parenting shortcomings, and validate their experiences and reactions.

(This cannot be overstated, in terms of setting things right with the people we've hurt, especially when those people are our children. But it's so hard to do, I know!)

And,

2.   STOP BEATING HERSELF UP!!

I explained to my respondent that she'd only parented the same way she'd been parented herself, and that I could guarantee it hadn't been anything like ideal. The key to getting things to move was to practise as much self-compassion as possible.

Why self-forgiveness is the key

So, this is what happened, in my correspondent's own words:

"I knew you were going to say to apologize to my children. And I know I need to do this. But emotionally I can't do it. It will hurt me too much to bring up past experiences. I don't think I have the emotional strength to apologize to them, on my own.

"I know I need to nullify my own *busha* if I want to get peace with this, and the *yetzer* hara is having a field day with me. For now, I will ask H-Shem for the strength to eventually do this, and ask H-Shem to allow my tefillot and teshuvot to be accepted, even though this situation with my children is hanging over me, especially since it is Elul."

One brave lady

My correspondent is one brave lady, because if you asked any single one of us if we'd be happy to say sorry to our kids – particularly the kids we KNOW we haven't done a great job of parenting, and who have suffered a great deal as a result – I guarantee that none of us would be running over eagerly to get the whole apology party on the road.

Saying sorry is really, really hard. And it's harder still when we know we really screwed up; and it's harder still when we don't even know if our apology is going to be accepted, or if it's even going to 'fix' things the way we hope.

So then, what options are really left open to us, if we're somehow stuck knowing we need to say sorry, but unable to do it?

You know what I'm going to say next, don't you?

At that point, there is no other option on the table except to get God involved. And that's exactly what my correspondent did. Here's what she told me:

Get God involved, and see miracles

"I wanted to let you know the most amazing miracles happened to me today.

"I was in the middle of my Hitbodedut, when I started thinking that the same way that my children's situation, which is painful for me as a mother, is getting me closer to H-Shem, the situation is also there to get them closer to H-Shem, too.

"Don't get me wrong I'm not excusing myself for how I treated them strictly and harshly. But I'm starting to understand that, for whatever reason, I was the messenger for their test – for the tribulations they had to have - and it was much better that it came via me, who really does love them, then via some other route.

"This idea gave me permission to forgive myself, and took a huge load off my shoulders. I physically felt lighter, and more at peace with myself. Everything comes from H-Shem, and everything H-Shem does is good and for our own good.

"I know that I still need to apologize to them, but H-Shem will give me the strength to do so, at the right time.

"Later on, I was talking to my daughter when all of a sudden she started thanking me, telling me what a great mom I was to her growing up. I tried to apologize to her, but she said that there's nothing to apologize for. My husband was also there, and tried to say that we'd all made mistakes during those hard times, but she shushed him, and said 'let's just say I'm sorry to each other and start anew.'

"WOW!

"I'm still in amazing shock. THANK YOU H-SHEM, 1 MILLION TIMES OVER! If you think this story will bring chizzuk to others, please publicize this amazing miracle."

Her story certainly gave ME a lot of chizzuk...

Learning the lessons of forgiveness

There are so many things we could learn about true forgiveness from this story. When I was trying to pull it together into a coherent 'strategy of forgiveness', the following elements jumped out at me:

In order to really forgive, and in order to really apologise, we need the following things:

Honesty

Namely, to admit that we genuinely have done things wrong, and that we aren't perfect, even when that's very painful.

Remorse

To feel bad about our negative actions, and the consequences they had for the people in our lives, and to want to avoid repeating the same mistakes again in the future.

Hitbodedut

Talking to God about what we actually need to do, in order to fix the mess we made, as well as asking Him to give us the enormous emotional and spiritual strength required in order for us to own up to our faults.

Emuna – i.e., Ein Od Milvado, God set the whole situation up, and He had His reasons for doing that

This is where we start to see that we're not in control of our lives, and that often, we're kind of stuck playing a part that we don't particularly want or like. It also means that we see that the other people in our life who may have hurt us, are also just God's 'puppets', in a manner of speaking, and just coming to teach us some sort of lesson, or to right some sort of spiritual wrong that may not even be from this lifetime (just like what happened in the Baal Shem Tov story).

Self-forgiveness

All of these things are key, and all of them are part of the secret of true forgiveness. But if I had to pick one thing out of this list to emphasise, then self-forgiveness would be it.

Because:

> *If we can't forgive ourselves, we*
> *also can't sincerely forgive others.*
> *And if we can't forgive ourselves, we*
> *won't have the emotional strength*
> *required to fix what we broke, and*
> *to ask others for forgiveness.*

A quiet shabbat

So the big question for me on shabbat was this: go to the Kotel for Friday night prayers like I always do, or not?

Friday morning, I went for a long walk via Geula to Machane Yehuda to buy stuff for shabbat, and it seemed to me like something fundamental had changed in the atmosphere of Jerusalem. I know people were still being stabbed all over the place, but it suddenly felt much safer to be in the Holy City again.

As shabbat came in, we made the decision to go down to the Kotel to pray, as has become our custom over the past year. Last week, when it was still Sukkot, there was standing room only at the Wailing Wall. This week, it was the emptiest I've seen it for a long while, although still full of people, notably a whole bunch of soldiers and goyim.

The soldiers were dancing and singing their socks off, and the goyim were doing all sorts of weird prayer circles, chants and mumblings. I sat down to say my Tikkun Haklali (having dropped my kid off at her friend in the Jewish Quarter of the Old City) – and burst into tears. I don't know why.

I prayed, met my husband, collected my kid from her friend's house and walked back home. All quiet, uneventful and actually quite nice. My kid had a plan to meet her friend again the next day, and I agreed to walk her in.

Shabbat morning, I went to hear Rav Shalom Arush's shiur in the Chut Shel Chessed yeshiva, like I do some times, and I crossed Neviim street to go into Meah Shearim and on to the yeshiva. It was pretty quiet and almost deserted on the streets.

Just before the shiur started, the roads exploded with the sounds of sirens, and we all sat there looking at each other, as the Rav gave a very rousing shiur about how the test of today is to walk – everywhere – with God.

Rav Arush explained that the only thing that's going to protect us is God, and to turn our fear of stabbing Arab terrorists into fear of the Almighty instead. I came home feeling pretty calm, and filled-up by the Rav's words of wisdom and emuna, although still wondering about what had just happened to cause all the noise.

We ate lunch, and me and my daughter headed off to the Old City around 3pm, her to her friend and me to go and do some praying at the grave of King David. Again, it was *very* quiet going in. I dropped my daughter off in the Jewish Quarter, headed over to the Zion gate – and then got stuck there for 40 minutes because they weren't letting anyone out.

I said some Psalms, waited a bit, then went over to the Jaffa Gate – which the police had also blocked, and closed. Hmm. In the meantime, the sirens and the helicopters had started up again, and again I wondered what was going on, but I didn't feel the horrible fear and stress that was literally crippling me for most of last week, Baruch Hashem.

All the tourists were pulling out their huge i-Phones and scrolling up and down to see what was happening. 'Two people stabbed in Neveeem' someone said. 'Where's that?' their friend asked. Hmm. It's the road that's two minutes away from my house.

'Someone else just got stabbed at the Damascus Gate' someone else rejoined. Then one of the local Arab's joined in with the kicker: 'They just killed three soldiers!' he yelled out. Gulp!

And anyway, who's the 'they', o Arab shopkeeper?!

After a few more minutes, they started letting people through the barrier again (thank God, I've started waxing my eyebrows properly again, so no-one suspected me of being a terrorist...) and I came home in a very thoughtful mood.

Motzae shabbat, I checked the news, and saw that no-one had actually been killed by the terrorists, thank God, just wounded. The choppers are going crazy again overhead as I write this. Who knows what's going on now? But my fear levels have still reduced a lot from last week, thank God, and I'm starting to feel like the situation is cope-able again, even though people are still being stabbed on the streets every day.

I hope it lasts.

Seeking relief in Ikea

In London, Ikea was top of the list of places I hated going. I hated the traffic jams to get there, I hated the enormous crowd of people you had to fight through just to shop, and I REALLY hated the two hour wait to pay for your stuff and get the heck out of there.

Now, IKEA Israel has always been a much more pleasant experience than IKEA London ever was: much less traffic, much less barging and noise and best of all, the café is 100% glatt kosher... But to say that it's a 'relaxing' experience? Not really. Especially not when you discover that all the chatchkees you picked up for three Nis are costing you as much as a cruise to the Bahamas.

But yesterday, Thursday, I couldn't take it anymore. From where I am in Jerusalem, I think I hear every police car and ambulance being dispatched to every incident in the whole city. All day, I heard the multiple sirens and 'honking' sound that is the sure-fire sign that a terrorist has just struck again, and I sat there tensed to the max, waiting to get more details.

It's a little easier when everyone is at home and at least you're not actively worrying that your family could be directly affected, but one bunch of sirens exploded around coming home time for the kid who's in school in the Old City, and I felt so anxious, literally like I'd reached breaking point.

All week, I'd had severe tension headaches (that I usually never get), pains in my neck and throat, and a general all-over feeling of unwellness that I knew was stress-related. But how to stop stressing when you live in a very intense, albeit very holy place, and there's always something dangerous going on?

Physically and emotionally I was suffering from some severe Post Traumatic Stress Disorder, and I needed a break from the sirens. My 12 year old came home from school wearing her familiar panicked face and panting heavily (her sprinting has come on a treat since the latest outbreak of Arab violence...) and asked me if we could go to IKEA.

Usually, I will pull any trick in the book to avoid going to IKEA, even if it is glatt kosher, but yesterday I jumped at the chance to get some relief from the sirens and tension. As my friend remarked, 'no-one ever got stabbed in IKEA', and as my husband remarked, IKEA has no gold-effect furniture, so the Arabs don't shop there.

Perfect!

We got in the car (my husband came too) and set out for four hours of freedom from the madness. On the way back, I pondered on how crazy the world has got really, and how it's really become the *olam hafuch*, or 'upside-down world' they talk of in the Gemara. I mean, who ever went to *IKEA* to relax?

There are many signs that Moshiach is fast on the way, but when spending four hours in IKEA becomes a way of reducing your stress levels, you just know something fundamental has got warped out of place.

The calm before the storm

After Wednesday's twin terror attacks in Jerusalem, I went a bit weird and kind of shut down a little (I know I'm not alone...). It's kind of ironic that I'm currently reading a book called 'Does Stress Damage the Brain?', because all week I've definitely been proving its thesis. I forgot appointments I made to meet people, I couldn't concentrate or think straight, and Wednesday night I was so tired I crashed into bed at 9pm.

Stress, stress, stress.

What to do about it all? In terms of my life, our lives, here and now? What to do about it?

The terrorists aren't going away any time soon. They are just the big stick that God is using to wake us all up, and show our anti-Torah politicians and citizens that they're barking up the wrong tree.

Right now, there are armed guards on pretty much every corner of the Old City and its surroundings. My local makolet in Meah Shearim is selling pepper spray (under the counter, quietly...). My kids come home with stories about people being stabbed with scissors and screwdrivers and even, unbelievably, vegetable peelers. (I think that one is still an urban myth, but who knows).

On shabbat, Rav Arush said that we can't run away from God, and the answer is to walk with Hashem wherever we go. If we're walking with Hashem, we'll be OK. So now before I go out, I ask God to 'walk with me', and give me (and the rest of my family) a bodyguard of angels to escort us.

I asked my youngest, who goes to school in the Old City, how the rest of the kids in her class are doing. One hasn't left her house for two weeks (she only moved to the Old City in August, and is completely traumatized). She told me that another group of her friends, the ones that live in the City of David, are still walking to and from school by themselves, except now they have pepper spray. (A lot of the terrorists come from their neighborhood.)

They are doing 'relaxing' hour in school now, and giving them regular 'chizzuk' conversations after each new attack, along the lines of 'we aren't scared, and we aren't going to let the Arabs scare us!' One of the girls asked what she should do if she *was* actually still scared, despite all the chizzuk. They didn't really know what to tell her.

Yesterday, my husband came home with a few Likutey Moharans, that Rav Arush had given the yeshiva students to distribute for free. There's a Breslov tradition that having a copy of the Likutey Moharan on the shelf protects the home.

We heard a story first hand to prove that a little while ago, when one of my husband's acquaintances, a property manager, had a fire at one of his flats. Everything was destroyed except the room Rebbe Nachman's book was in, which was completely untouched – the clothes in the cupboard didn't even smell smoky.

So that's my recipe for dealing with the mega terrorist-induced stress this week:

» Walk with God everywhere you go

» Get a copy of Likutey Moharan for your home

» Do a lot of praying

"Can I buy pepper spray?"

Is what my 12 year old asked me yesterday. Apparently, lots of the girls in her school now have their own canister, and my kid was up on all the different prices and sizes, and wanted me to get her a 'one ounce-er'.

Apart from the craziness of having a discussion about buying pepper spray for my 12 year old daughter, there's another, additional level of craziness going on here: namely that anyone thinks that pepper spray actually works.

Yes, I know in theory that if anyone dodgy comes anywhere close it would be useful to spritz them with something nasty in the face and run off. But in practice, people don't react with that much presence of mind when confronted by a knife-wielding terrorist. The usual response is stunned shock and temporary paralysis, not a lightning-fast reflex to grab the pepper spray and start squirting it around.

My other daughter told me a first-hand account she heard about one of the attempted stabbings in the Old City, when an Arab *woman* attacked two Jewish men. She first stabbed one, and he fell to the floor. The other one was carrying a laptop in his hand, and he used that to smash the terrorist in the face.

Now, you'd think that ordinarily a strong man smashing a woman in the face with anything would be the end of the story. Not in this case. The *female* terrorist had her nose broken the first time he hit her with the laptop, but she stood back up and tried to stab him again. He hit her a second time, and it didn't stop her from trying to stab him again. A third time, and she was still coming after him with the knife.

At that point, the wounded man mumbled to his friend to shoot her – with the gun he'd had in his possession the whole time, but forgot he had. He did just that, and wounded the terrorist non-fatally.

Now, both these guys had been through the army, they'd both been in combat situations, most recently in Gaza, and they knew how to handle themselves in dangerous situations. If that's the best they could do when a *female* terrorist attacked them, what hope do the rest of us have, even if we're lugging around a huge canister of pepper spray?

The more this stressful saga continues, the more I'm seeing that there really is only God to rely on, and nothing else. Sure, take the gun, take the pepper spray, spend hours figuring out how you're going to scream, lunge, run away fast, kick the attacker in the goolies etc. but remember that God is really the deciding factor in all these things, not human prowess, proficiency with firearms, muscles, or anything else.

In the meantime, I'm not buying the pepper spray for my daughter. That might change in the future, but right now that seems to be where I'm holding. If I *really* thought it would help protect her, I'd do it in a heart-beat. But my soul is whispering to me that pepper spray is a broken reed, and that I'd do much better relying on God 100% to protect my family, and not feeling 'safer' just because I got my kid a one ounce-er.

After the headlines have faded

The last few months, any lingering love affair I still had with the news has died a fast death. I've been broadly 'news-free' for about 8 years, give or take, and I haven't missed it all. But with the recent upswing in violence here in Israel, I've been reading more news headlines than I have done for years.

Usually, I only check after I hear a bunch of sirens, and thank God, it's been much quieter in my neck of the woods this week. But two weeks' back, I logged on the apparently 'frum' website Arutz 7 the day after the terrible double murder of Aharon Bennett and Rabbo Nechemia Lavi in the Old City. I was shocked to my core to see that they were offering video footage of Rabbi Lavi being stabbed to death as the 'Editor's Pick'.

I know, we're all so used to the 'bread and circuses' approach of modern society that we don't bat an eyelid any more at how voyeuristic, callous and un-Jewish all this 'live action video' actually is.

Let me ask you something: how would you feel if your dad, or your husband, or your son, got viciously stabbed to death, and then the next day your friends and neighbors (or worse, your kids' school-friends) were busy watching it on their i-Phones. How would you feel?

I was pondering this a lot recently, because while the headlines have ebbed, and the families of Aharon Bennett and Rabbi Nechemia Lavi have faded back into relative obscurity, the real impact that these real tragedies had on these real people continue.

Even though millions of people are watching them on the internet, the victims of the of terrorists aren't film stars being paid to play the part, just to entertain us and give us something to blog about, and to talk about, and to share on Facebook. They are real human beings.

Let me tell you a little bit about what's happened to family Lavi, now that things have gone 'back to normal'. Before her husband was stabbed to death on his own doorstep, Mrs Lavi was a teacher in my daughter's school in the Old City. She's left that job now, because the family couldn't bring themselves to move back to their home in the Old City after the shiva, and have now moved to Bet El, to be close to both sets of parents.

Many of the kids have had to move school, as it's too far to travel back and forwards to Jerusalem every day.

That murder that people were gawking at online didn't just kill a beloved Abba and husband; it threw eight people's lives into complete disarray. The family effectively lost their dad, lost their home, lost their jobs and sources of income, lost their community and lost their whole way of life – all at once.

Of course, that's not deemed 'newsworthy', so you won't be reading about that any time soon as you scroll through the latest headlines. And that's why I hate the news, and I hate all the mileage that people are making in the blogosphere out of the ongoing tragedies occurring here, and also elsewhere.

This stuff is not just fodder for more opinion pieces, more speculation, more breathless, excited, giddy posting about the 'latest'. The impact of the headlines that are so quickly made, shared and forgotten can and does last a lifetime on the people involved.

And if we forget that, and we get caught up in chasing the drama instead of remembering the tragedy, that bodes very badly for us and our collective humanity and caring.

 # 'Either Moshiach really is coming, or I'm going mad...' #

You'd be amazed how many of my conversations are starting like that at the moment (OK, if you read my blog regularly, maybe you won't be so amazed). Things are pretty calm in Jerusalem at the moment, thanks to 400 security guards posted on pretty much every corner of town. But there's still a sense, at least in my home, that it's the calm before the storm, and that 'something' is in the offing.

I've had those feelings before, and often they were answered by a mini-war in Gaza, or something similar. I've also occasionally had those feelings before, and nothing happened. I was on *shpilkes* for weeks, and then the tension and pressure kind of faded without any obvious release.

So who knows what's really going on, but I feel pretty weird for no obvious reason. Like I said, either Moshiach really is coming, or I'm going mad. I guess time will tell which one it was.

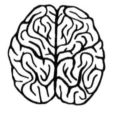

How $3 miraculously bought a week's groceries

Between davening mincha and maariv in shul, my husband overhead the following story:

One of the men in shul was telling his friend how he'd been in the supermarket, when he accidentally bumped into another person's trolley. He hadn't been concentrating (you'll see why in a minute) – and during his daydreaming, he'd accidentally gone into the back of the person who'd stopped in front of him.

His fellow shopper went ballistic and started yelling and cursing at him loudly at the top of his voice, causing him no end of embarrassment as everyone else in the shop gathered round to see what was going on.

All the first man had in his trolley was a loaf of bread, and the man he'd bumped into started screaming at him that he didn't even need a trolley, if all he could afford to put in it was a loaf of bread!!!

At this point, the first man broke down a little, and stiffly explained that he didn't have a lot of money to put a lot of other things in his trolley....

At that point, something softened in the other shopper, and he started apologizing for all the nasty things he'd just said, and all the criticism he'd heaped on his head. The first man accepted his apology, but still looked pretty down and broken-hearted. The second shopper now had a complete change of heart and decided to make some real teshuva.

He told the first man that he was going to fill up his trolley and pay for it all, to say sorry for abusing him in public and drawing attention to the fact that he didn't have a lot of money. He literally dragged the first shopper round the supermarket, piling as many things as he could into the trolley.

Good as his word, he paid the whole bill when it came to more than 800nis (around $230) patted the first shopper on the back, and then carried on with his own grocery run. A little later, the second man came out of the supermarket and spotted the first shopper sitting down on a bench, crying.

He came over to him and asked him: 'Why are you crying? I made it up to you now, didn't I?' The first shopper nodded, and explained what was going on:

'A little while ago, my wife told me we had no food in the house,' he said. 'All I had in my pocket was 10 Nis (around $2.50), but I told my wife that I would got to the supermarket in any case, and that Hashem would help me. And He did.'

How does God want us to live?

A little while back, my husband and I went into the Old City to do a bit of praying by the Wall, and to grab a bite to eat. That's not such a big deal – we've been going to the Kotel pretty much most Friday nights for over a year, and my daughter goes to school in the Old City, so I've been driving in and out of there for a month now.

But this was the first time in a few weeks that we actually spent some time there. We got our shwarma, found a table to sit at outside in the main square, and then had to spend the next half an hour listening to some older Anglo woman complaining loudly into her cellphone about all the people who were 'living in a dream' around her.

"These people are crazy! They're letting their two year olds play outside by themselves! [In the completely pedestrianized Hurva Square in the center of the Jewish Quarter.] There's no policemen here, no security, nothing! Anything could happen! I can't believe what's going on here and no-one is taking me seriously. I complain and complain but no-one makes a move to come back to me.'

I'd had enough of hearing her moaning after a minute, but sadly, she kept on going and even outlasted my shwarma.

I walked down to the Kotel afterwards, and I pondered that woman and her hyper-vigilance, and hyper-anxiety about the situation, and her hyper-criticism of the people who weren't just cowering in their basements or walking around with armed guards.

Is that life? Is that really how God wants us to live?

OK, sure, I know things are a little crazy right now, and that I'm driving my kid to school instead of letting her walk like usual, but there comes a point where quality of life in the here and now has to trump quantity of life.

I've just finished reading Bernie Siegel's 'Love, Medicine and Miracles', and it's one of the best and most uplifting spiritual books I've ever read, despite being full of death and cancer.

One of the themes that Siegel, a busy surgeon who had an epiphany 30 years' back that attitude, emotions and soul were much more powerful healing forces than anything 'medical' he could offer his patients, underlines again and again that life shouldn't be measured in years; it should be measured in happiness.

Rav Levi Yitzhak Bender said the same, when he commented: 'You may only live a little, but live it well and make it nice!'

Siegel saw patient after patient hating their life, and looking at their incurable disease as the 'out'. He also saw patient after patient having their life unnaturally extended by all sorts of horrific medical interventions, instead of being able to die naturally and at peace, surrounded by their loved ones.

(I'm not a halachic authority, and I'm not going to get into the whole 'right to die' debate, but what I can tell you is that Rebbe Nachman was really against doctors and medicine and he advised his followers to avoid both completely, as much as possible.)

One of the things Bernie Siegel used to ask his patients is: "If you knew today was your last day, how would you live it? What would you change?"

It's a question for all of us. I sat in the Jewish Quarter listening to the unhappy, hyper-critical 'concerned citizen' and I wondered what she'd be doing with her time if she knew today was the last day of her life. I asked myself the same thing – and it was the first time that I can remember being thrilled that I'd spent far more time writing than tidying up my house and hanging laundry.

I asked my husband that question, and he immediately snapped out of his funny mood, and found something more productive to do with his time.

Our sages say that we should make teshuva the day before we die, which practically means we have to live as though every day is our last, because maybe it is. Yes, there's a place for precaution and soldiers on street corners, but in our modern world there's too much emphasis placed on length of days, and nowhere near enough put on amount of happiness.

If you knew today was your last day, what would you do differently?

Slow down, girl

That's the message God has been trying to give me for months already, but I keep kind of ignoring him. Every time I realize I really do need to slow down a bit, some other crisis or issue erupts, or some other idea takes root in my brain and I feel compelled to get on with it before, well, 'the end'.

That's how it's been for years, actually, that I'm rushing to get everything done before 'the end', presumably when Moshiach shows up, and redemption occurs, and all my answering activities on Quora grind to a halt.

But the last week or two, I've been having this strange idea that maybe, just maybe, it's possible for at least some of my main issues to get resolved without Moshiach doing it for me. That notion, bizarre and alien as it first sounded when it popped into my head a little while ago, is actually helping me to get quite a few things 'unstuck', while at the same time encouraging me to slow down.

How's it doing that?

Well, for the first time in ages I'm actually starting to think in terms of beyond next week. I've been living in this Moshiach-ready crazy reality where he really is coming – if not today, then tomorrow. And if not tomorrow, then it definitely has to be by the end of the month. On the one hand, this belief has paralyzed me from doing things I really should be getting on with (like arranging braces for my kids, or starting to think about how to buy my own home again, without Moshiach-induced open miracles).

And on the other, it's been a harsh taskmaster, screaming at me to publish four books already, and write 10,000 words a week while I've still got a computer and electricity...

But I can't carry on like that, by turns pressured and working like a lunatic, or apathetic and trapped, waiting for God and Moshiach to resolve all of my issues. I have to live in the here and now. I have to believe that life will continue for a good while yet. I have to stop holding my breath on the one hand, and stop ceaselessly cramming in more and more things on the other.

I have to slow down, so that I can actually start to get some stuff that doesn't involve my keyboard done.

That much is becoming clear to me. How I actually go about doing this is still hidden in the mists. I'll continue asking God for some clues and guidance; I'll practice trying to stay off my computer at least some of the time; and I'll hope that God will show me how I can really be the 'me' He wants me to be, just the calmer, more productive and more relaxed version who believes that even though Moshiach really might still come tomorrow, that's not the end of the world as we know it, but actually just the beginning.

Back to the Baba Sali

After 10 years, God finally arranged for us to get a new car again. The old Getz had racked up hundreds of thousands of kilometers, and served us very well down the years, but as it's windscreen wipers got ever-more squeaky, and it's steering got even more clunky and heavy to maneuver, about six months ago I stopped wanting to drive it.

What that meant is that trips to the Baba Sali, that used to be a monthly if not a weekly staple before I moved to Jerusalem, all but stopped.

But last week, we took delivery of our new, leasehold i20 set of wheels, and I knew its first real trip had to be a visit to the Baba Sali, in Netivot. So today, I set out with a friend who'd never been to the Baba Sali's tomb, and we headed down South.

You should know something about the Baba Sali and me: I had a bad car crash there a couple of years' back that sparked a chain of events that ended with me selling my house and moving to Jerusalem (and also caused a massive nervous breakdown, but that's a story for another time.)

The last time I went to the Baba Sali, a few months' back, I also got into a minor car crash. We were trying to find the way to our daughter's new school, and kept getting completely lost and driving past the exit for Netivot. The third time it happened, I told my husband we should just go visit the Baba Sali already, and while we were sitting at the lights deliberating on what to do, someone rear-ended us. (Did I mention that the Baba Sali has a sense of humor?)

After we'd got our crash out the way, it was a no-brainer to take the detour and make the trip.

The Baba Sali's grave is probably one of my favorite holy sites in the whole of Israel: I know this sounds a little strange, as I'm actually describing a graveyard, but it's one of the most vibrant, 'alive' places you'll ever visit. There's always people there celebrating some simcha or other, screaming into their phones that they're 'By the Baba Sali!', trying to stuff their homemade cake into your face, or BBQing up a storm in the outside area next to the tomb.

Man, it's a party place in the best sense, and I love being there - but since my crash, I'm always a little wary of the drive there and back.

So I got there, settled myself in to my usual spot, and started to feel instantly calmer and just 'good' again. Life was good. Everything's good. I'm good. Baruch Hashem, my family's good. I got a few insights into a few of the more taxing issues I'm dealing with at the moment, and I also got a nudge from a big poster on the wall to stop talking on my mobile on the street.

Apparently, some big poskim have come out to say that it's not a tznius thing to do, and should be avoided at all costs. One of the things I came to pray on was that I should manage to be more tznius now I'm back in the 'real world' again, so I was happy to find something small that I could try to do, to show God that I still want to do better than I am.

I collected my friend, drove out of the Baba Sali's compound, and made my way back to the highway. On the way out of Netivot, this white cat suddenly appeared at the side of the road, and proceeded to stroll very slowly straight in front of my car.

The cat committed suicide. There's no other way of describing it.

I tried to brake a little, but I was going so fast (but still legally...) that slamming on the brakes could have caused an accident, and risking human injury to save a cat didn't seem like a good idea.

So the cat died, and I sat in the car a little unnerved, wondering what 'the message' was with this latest car incident involving a visit to the Baba Sali (as far as I remember, I've never killed a cat, or any other animal, while driving.)

Suddenly, I got it: slow down!

The same message I've been getting again and again and again, recently.

Slow down! Live life a little more, savor it, stop rushing everywhere and thinking the world is going to end tomorrow.

So I'm trying to do that, even more than I was. It's a shame the cat had to buy the farm to give me that clue a little louder than usual, but clearly it had its own *tikkun* going on. How I actually slow down without causing a pile-up, I still don't know. But BH, I'm planning to go back to Netivot soon, and I hope to get more guidance then that won't involve my car in any way, shape or form.

Some thoughts on the French terrorist attacks

Yesterday, a big chunk of the Old City walls next to the Jaffa Gate were lit up in the French Tricolor colors of red, white and blue. Part of me thought 'that's cool!', and then the other part of me thought: 'what's wrong with us, that we're falling all over ourselves to suck up to the French like this?!'

Now, I'm not a political creature, and this isn't going to be a whole big diatribe against politicians or international machinations, but I found the whole 'French flag wall-thing' pretty disturbing on a few levels, not least that it was amazing how fast Jerusalem City Hall arranged the whole thing.

I mean, it's taken me three trips to the town hall just to get a replacement parking sticker for my car, so I'm pretty impressed with how fast they moved to fix the lighting system and get all the French flags put up on the lamp-posts on Jerusalem's main drags.

(They were probably left over from the equally slick 'Je suis Charlie' Jerusalem campaign, which saw City Hall draped in a massive canvas stating it's solidarity with the French after the Charlie Hebdo massacre. That also unnerved me, because it seemed we were making more of a fuss over the dead goyim than we were about the dead Jews.)

So vague uneasiness about the 'slickness' of the whole French solidarity thing aside, what else have I been thinking about the French terrorist attacks? The answer is: not very much. Yes, it's shocking and disturbing on one level – but the simple fact is that I don't live in France, so the pre-shabbat attack near Otniel was far more upsetting to me.

Like so many of the other olim that have moved to Israel from Europe in recent years, me and my family saw the writing on the wall years' ago. I spent the best part of a decade trying to convince people (particularly Jewish people) to at least start *wanting* to move to Israel. At this point, I am so fried out by all the 'terrorism', and all the 'drama', and all the craziness going on in the world, that it's got to the point that I'm not really paying it all that much attention.

I got my Islamic terrorism message loud and clear 10 years' ago when the London tube was bombed, and we moved to Israel less than a month later. Now, if the 'situation' is literally on my doorstep (and sadly, it often really is), I'll sit up and take notice. If it's not – I can no longer spare the time, energy and strength required to panic about, agonize over, or ruminate upon things that are happening thousands of miles away.

I did a whole bunch of that stuff for years' already, and now I need a rest.

God is running the world, God is good and everything that happens contains a tailored, specific message for change and improvement for each and every one of us. We can't live other people's lives, make their decisions, or read their runes for them. People thought we were crazy for leaving the 'comfort' and easy money lifestyle of the UK, and maybe we were.

Only time will tell if they are crazy for staying put.

As God went to great pains to tell the prophets thousands of years' ago, He doesn't want people to die, He wants them (us...) to make teshuva.

What happened in France is just another shot across the bows that the God-less status quo is about to collapse, and that people have a choice: to cling on to God and our holy Tzaddikim, or not.

Beyond that, what's really left to say?

False prophets (and how to spot a real one)

In this time of geula blog madness, false prophets are still very much a 'live' issue for the Jewish people.

On the one side, we have terrible, blood-curdling predictions, and on the other, we have reassuring if concerned statements from our true Tzaddikim that the situation is indeed grave, but that teshuva, tefilla and tzedaka can still sweeten everything.

With all the millions of pundits out there, Jewish and otherwise, who are 'predicting' things all the time, we really need some help to work out which modern-day 'prophets' are actually the real deal, and worth listening to, and which aren't.

Enter the Rambam. According to the Rambam, an individual needs to have the following qualities in order to qualify as a 'potential true prophet':

1. Deep wisdom

2. Broad-minded knowledge

3. The ability to be in control of his or her physical urges, as well as to be unaffected by the vanities of the material world.

4. The prophet-in-waiting has to be involved in holy pursuits at all times.

According to the Rambam, a prophet also has to prepare themselves very carefully before they receive the flow of Divine information, and they have to be in a state of absolute joy, because: "Prophecy does not come to one who is sad or lazy."

So what does it all mean, when we're trying to figure out which pundit to believe, and which blog post to stress about? Let's take a deeper look at the Rambam's criteria for who is a 'true prophet', and who couldn't be in a million years.

True prophets:

Have deep wisdom

Deep wisdom doesn't mean someone once read a book of kabbalah, had a funny dream, can translate Hebrew to English (or vice-versa) or correctly predicted who was going to win Israel's last elections.

Have broad-minded knowledge

Finding allusions to the latest autistic pronouncements in the latest Brad Pitt film they just watched doesn't count as 'broad-minded knowledge'. (By way of comparison, the sages of the Sanhedrin had to know 70 languages, and be whizzes at math, logic and natural science before they'd even be considered for a place.)

Have the ability to control their physical urges, and be unaffected by the material world

Any wannabe-prophet who is giving over their 'nevua' via Facebook, or who has their own twitter account, is clearly not meeting these requirements.

Are involved in holy pursuits at all times

It was only when I got to Jerusalem and I saw really holy people in action, and the humility they have, and the utter simplicity and sweetness they have, and the lack of arrogance and superiority they evince, that the penny dropped that Rabbis with their own YouTube channel, blog, Facebook accounts and personal agenda to be the next Moshiach are simply not anywhere near the same playing field, kedusha-wise.

That doesn't mean you can't be holy, and still doing good work online, or still be holy and coaching little league, or visiting chocolate factories, or riding horses in your spare time. But it definitely does mean that you aren't in the really big leagues when it comes to kedusha, where the potential prophets are hanging out.

Prepare themselves rigorously, to get prophecies

Real prophets don't just get some half-baked idea while doing the washing up that WW3 is starting tomorrow. They also don't have vague dreams of seeing Obama riding a white donkey into Jerusalem (unless they spent the 40 days prior to having that dream fasting and praying in the desert somewhere...)

Need to be happy

And this, dear reader, is where so many of today's false internet prophets are really falling down. When a bona fide Tzaddik says 'trouble's brewing' you can believe they aren't just scaremongering or going on a power trip so fifty people will comment on their post.

The only time they say hard things is in order to get us to make the teshuva we need to turn things around. So buyer beware! Just because someone thinks they may be a prophet, doesn't mean we should actually treat them like one.

Stop the world

So, you remember how I keep getting messages to slow down and stop rushing around all the time? There's just one problem: I'm finding it almost impossible to do that. Every week, I have so many things to get done, or deal with, or sort out, across all fronts.

One week, it was sorting out the new parking permit for our car (which if you know anything about Israeli bureaucracy, you'll also know that's a full time job in and of itself). Then, it was sorting out all the books etc. that my kid needed when she started her new school, and trying to settle down into the new routine that involved. (You'll find out why she was moving school in the middle of the year a little later on.)

Then, my husband's back went out for a fortnight, which showed me that he actually does a whole lot more useful things around the house (and in our life generally) than I usually give him credit for.

Then, there was the world-wide Tikkun Haklali rally that I so wanted to get to, but in the end I ran out of time and energy, so I just ended up saying the Tikkun Haklali on my couch at home.

It was also *Chodesh Irgun*, which is this really dumb idea adopted by all Israeli youth groups to have a whole month of activities, culminating in a week where no-one (parents and children both) really sleeps more than two hours a night. By the end of the month everyone is frothing at the mouth from sleep deprivation.

And let's not even talk about THE BOOK that was meant to be out two weeks' ago already, and is still going through iteration after iteration. My amazing designer had a nervous breakdown last month, leaving me high and dry with the book 95% done, until I could find someone to finish it off.

Baruch Hashem, I found someone, but then they're using a different version of the software... and their designer only speaks Hebrew...and their email inexplicably crashed for most of last week, which meant they didn't get most of my emails, and I wasn't getting their emails, either.

Long story short, hard as I try to take it easy, God seems to still be piling on the pressure, in all sorts of small, time-consuming ways.

What can I say except: Baruch Hashem!!

I have no idea why I have to wake up at the crack of dawn feeling like I've got the next leg of my three million mile marathon to run today, but what I can tell you is that there are two things that are keeping me within touching distance of staying sane:

- » **Shabbat.** I simply have no idea how people who don't keep Shabbat can function in 2015.
- » **Hitbodedut** (personal prayer). I've started trying to talk to God for a few hours at a go, once a week, while I clean some of my house, and it's pretty much the only time I feel like a calm human being.

Clearly, 'pressure' is the theme *du jour*, as even my kids are feeling harassed, and having nervous breakdowns about all the things they have to get done this week.

I know there's an idea that if it doesn't kill us, it makes us stronger. That's a comforting thought once you're out the other end of the process, but in the meantime I'm just hoping it doesn't kill me first.

Temple time

The other day, I was listening to Shlomo Katz in the car, when he started singing these words: 'On the holiest day of the year, the holiest man in the world would enter the holiest place; and he would say the holiest name.'

He was talking about the Kohen HaGadol's Yom Kippur service in the temple. Just then, I came round the bend in the road I was driving inside the Old City, and the golden dome of Omar's Mosque hit me full in the face. For a few seconds, all I could think about was the temple, and how we Jews are missing it so much, without even realizing it.

Just think of this: you could drag the most crazy person in the community off to the temple, give them the fattest bull you could find to slaughter as an atonement – and that person would come out of that temple service a caring and empathetic human being again, maybe for the first time in their lives.

Man, we so need the temple, and the atonement and peace it could bring to all the troubled souls wandering around today.

Part of the reason I was having 'temple envy' is because I've also been trying to find one of my kids a new school. It's one thing to have demented lunatics trying to stab you on the way to school every day (God forbid), but it's another thing entirely when you get to school only to find that demented lunatics have taken over the classroom, too.

I'm not going to spell out in detail what's been going on, but suffice to say it got to a point that I didn't know which situation – the outer threat of physical violence, or the inner threat of emotional and spiritual violence - was really more scary or damaging.

I was praying on it for weeks and weeks, unsure whether to try to move my kid (again...) or just try to tough it out, and wait for the Arabs to calm down a bit, and the 'difficult person' in school to really cross the line, and get kicked-out by other parents with less patience and more gumption (and protektzia).

In the end, God forced my hand: my daughter got suspended for three days for complaining too loudly about the fact that she had six exams coming up in the next two weeks.

In most schools in Israel, you usually have to be caught doing hard drugs in the school toilets to get suspended, and even then it's not automatic. My usually calm, level-headed husband tried to sort things out – and came off the phone foaming at the mouth and gnashing his teeth.

I've watched him stay calm around some of the most crazy-making people you'll ever meet in your life, so his reaction to a five minute 'dose' of the difficult person was very instructive.

But moving school is so hard!

For a few more days I was in an agony of indecision, unsure what to do, or how to even do it. I decided to go and have a long chat with God about it all, and at the end of that I got the message loud and clear: get your kid out as soon as possible.

But to where?

Next thing I know, my daughter starts telling me about this newish school in a different neighbourhood that she'd be happy to go to. One of her friends from class had already moved there, and another friend was also ready to switch, but wanted someone to come with her.

Long story short, we went, we had the interview, she sat the tests, and she starts tomorrow, together with her good friend from class.

A miracle! Thanks, God!

But it's still scary to move. And it's even scarier to tell the 'difficult person' in the old school that we're leaving. Part of me feels so sorry for her, because I know she's so hard on others because she's so hard on herself, too. But I couldn't risk her doing any more serious damage to my kid's soul and self-esteem.

This generation only kicks against harsh punishments, cruel words and power trips – and God made it that way, because 'harsh discipline' is not the Torah-true way of educating our children. It always should have been 'education with love', but in this generation education with love is not a luxury – it's the ONLY way to relate to our kids.

In the meantime, I think about all the children, all the adults, who have been so fundamentally warped and damaged by all the criticism, harshness, anger, shame and blame they've experienced growing up, and it makes me very sad.

Only the temple can really fix this mess. I hope God gives it back to us soon.

Getting to grips with Rav Ovadia Yosef, ztl

Before his passing in 2013, I didn't know much more about Rav Ovadia Yosef than that he always wore sunglasses, and that he was the spiritual head of the Sephardi-charedi Israeli political party Shas, that served the interests of the *frum* Sephardi world.

After his death, more than 850,000 people turned out for his funeral in Jerusalem, which temporarily closed the capital down for the rest of the day. I happened to be on one of the last buses headed out of Jerusalem just before the funeral, and all the way down to the Mevasseret turnoff on Route 1, there was one coachload of mourners after another, driving up to pay their last respects.

In the weeks that followed, even the secular papers were full of stories recounting Rav Ovadia's selflessness, generosity, kindness, humility and vast Torah knowledge. Over the course of his lifetime, Rav Ovadia had been a staunch defender of the Torah world, and particularly the needs of his Sephardi brethren, and his sometimes uncompromising idealism had earned him a lot of enemies and detractors, particularly in the political sphere.

So much slander got spread around about the Rav in his lifetime, but when almost a million people made the effort to turn out for his funeral, it finally put those lies to rest, as story after story surfaced about how Rav Ovadia had sacrificed so much of his time, effort and even own meagre funds to help his fellow Jews.

Often, they were people who were at the lowest rung of Israeli society, like the new Sephardi immigrants who often arrived penniless from their Arab home states, and then found that the virulently secular Ashkenazi ruling elite in Israel was not exactly pleased to have a bunch of poor, religious people turn up on their doorstep.

The Sephardim faced a great deal of antagonism and outright abuse from the Israeli establishment, who went to great pains to tear them and their children away from their 'primitive, outmoded' religious traditions.

Into this chaotic swirl of hardship and suffering, stepped Rav Ovadia Yosef. Rav Ovadia's own family had immigrated to Israel from Iraq around the turn of the century. His father has brought a fortune with him, but was swindled out of it by a dishonest business partner, plunging the family into crushing poverty.

Even though Rav Ovadia was a childhood prodigy in Torah learning (he was regularly learning with, and teaching, men more than three times his age, by the tender age of 10) his family's financial circumstances forced his father to pull his precocious son out of the Porat Yosef Yeshiva in the Old City, to come and help him with his grocery store.

When his teachers found their star pupil missing from lessons, they went to visit the father to enquire where he was. Once they realized what the problem was, one of Rav Ovadia's rebbes told his father that *he* would work in the store, instead of the young prodigy, for two hours a day, so that Rav Ovadia's learning shouldn't be interrupted.

Even though his star started rising from a very young age in the Torah world, life was anything but easy for young Ovadia, and his new bride Margalit. The couple were married in Jerusalem in 1944, when the devastation being wreaked by World War 2 was still in full swing.

For the first 20 years' of their married life, the Ovadias lived in abject poverty, barring a three year stint when Rav Ovadia accepted the post of deputy Chief Rabbi of Egypt, between 1947-50.

The Ovadias moved around frequently during that time, spending a few years in Petah Tikvah, and also in Tel Aviv, where Rav Ovadia started to gain much wider fame when he accepted a position as the Sephardic Rav of Tel Aviv.

Everywhere he went he continued to study Torah at every opportunity, to teach Torah to anyone who wanted to learn, and to try to improve the lot of the Sephardim in Eretz Yisrael. By the time Rav Ovadia become the spiritual leader of the Shas political party at the age of 62, he'd already accomplished more than most people achieve in twenty lifetimes.

By the end of his life in 2013, Rav Ovadia had authored more than 50 books of halachic responsa, and he'd became the undisputed Torah decisor of the generation. His approach to making a ruling was to comb through all the many different sources available, find a consensus approach, and then to apply that logic to present day issues and difficulties.

While Rav Ovadia's approach to Torah was one of impeccable scholarship and respect for halacha, his responsa were characterized by compassion and wherever possible, leniency. He tried to make the Torah as easy for people to follow as possible, without ever compromising it – which was not an easy feat, especially in a world where pressure was mounting to find 'solutions' to things like insincere conversions, illegitimate children (not children born out of wedlock, but children who were the result of an adulterous relationship etc.), and agunot, or 'chained' wives, whose husbands had either disappeared or were refusing to give them a get.

As each challenge was presented to Rav Ovadia, he went back to his 40,000 books (most of which he knew by heart) and poured over them until he found a halachically-acceptable response. But he always remembered that he wasn't just dealing with dry laws, he was dealing with people's lives, and he felt the pain of those who turned to him for help and clarity acutely.

Biographies of Jewish leaders are nearly always inspiring and uplifting, but often also a little unreal and 'too perfect'. There's an understandable tendency to gloss-over their challenges and personal difficulties, and to magnify their almost super-human achievements. Rav Ovadia was so well-known, and his battles were so often fought in the public arena, that in many ways, his biography just levelled the playing field by telling us more about his tremendous achievements and abilities.

He wasn't just the sunglasses-wearing leader of Shas; he was a man who from his early youth literally put everything he had on the line to further the cause of Torah in Eretz Yisrael, and to help out his fellow Jew. His message to the next generation was clear: Don't think that only an 'Ovadia Yosef' can make such a big difference to the world! Every Jew can do the same, if they only want to enough.

Whisper it quietly, but I really enjoyed this Artscroll Biography of Rav Ovadia – so much so that I finished it in one sitting. I didn't come away feeling bad that I don't know 40,000 Torah books by heart, or that I'm not 'Gadol HaDor' material. I came away knowing that every single Jew can make a massive difference in the world, including me. And that's something that every single one of us occasionally needs reminding about.

Musings on melaveh malka

A few years' back, my husband heard a class about the importance of melaveh malka, aka the 'fourth meal' that escorts the Shabbat Queen out of the mundane world on Saturday night. The Rav that gave it was a humble, realistic sort, and he explained how in his family, they would celebrate melaveh malka with a bar of chocolate, with each person eating a square *'lichvod Melaveh Malka'* (in the honor of melaveh malka).

That sounded like such a cool, simple-to-do idea that from that week on, me and my husband also started to do melaveh malka, albeit in a very, very simple way. One time, I was talking to someone about my simple Melaveh Malka, and trying to encourage them to do something similar when they told me flat out that "if you don't wash for bread, your melaveh malka doesn't count for anything". I was stung.

I knew that the Rav who'd taught my husband was a very learned halachic authority, so I couldn't believe he'd have either deliberately mislead his students, or got the halacha so obviously wrong. So I had my husband look it up in the Shulchan Aruch, and there it was in black and white: While washing for bread was clearly preferable, it was also acceptable to do Melaveh Malka even on something as simple as a piece of fruit.

This isn't the first time I came up against what I'll call the *'hyper-machmir'* all-or-nothing mindset that actually destroys the joy of the mitzvoth, and is rooted in a very subtle, but incredibly pernicious form of arrogance and superiority.

Rebbe Nachman himself was always dead-set against *chumrot*, or religious stringencies. He counselled his followers to strive to keep the basic laws to the best of their ability (all the time recognizing that even *that* was an incredible feat) – and to restrict their *chumrot* as much as possible. Rebbe Nachman advised that if you wanted, you could pick one mitzvah, and choose to try to keep that with all its additional practices and adornments. But everything else should be done with complete simplicity, and without any extra-strict practices.

Rebbe Nachman said these things more than 200 years' ago, when the general level of communal kedusha and mitzvah observance was so much higher than it is today. Rebbe Nachman could see what was coming down the pipe, because he also remarked that at the end of days, a man who washed his hands according to the halacha would be as unique in his generation as the Baal Shem Tov.

Spirituality has never been easy, but at this stage in history, when God so often appears to be buried under piles of materialism, minutiae, and arrogant ideas about impressing other people with the external form of the mitzvahs we do, it sometimes feels impossible to tap into the underlying meaning of all these things.

God wants the heart.

Sure, if I could wash for bread every *motzae Shabbat*, and spend the next two hours singing melaveh malka songs with my family, I'm pretty sure God would like that (as long as that's something I was doing *sincerely*, and not just to prove how 'frum' I was.) As it is, God knows that sometimes, even getting the food cooked for Shabbat is like climbing Mount Everest for me.

But I still want to do melaveh malka, in some quiet way. So I hope that when I have my cup of tea and cookie and call it a 'melaveh malka', God digs my melaveh malka as much as I do.

Sharing a beautiful vision

Nineteen year old Tehilla was born blind.

Her parents didn't want their daughter to grow up feeling like a second-class citizen, so despite her disability they decided that she should go to a 'normal' school, and be with 'normal' kids. It was very challenging logistically, but mostly OK – until the age of 10, when a former friend of Tehilla started mocking her for being blind and turning the class against her.

Cut to the core, Tehilla spent many weeks and months trying to pick herself up off the floor, but the damage done by mockery and malicious gossip can sometimes take a lifetime to heal. Eventually, with the encouragement of her family and a lot of prayer and emuna, the young Tehilla pulled herself together, stopped crying and tried to carry on.

But being a blind girl in a class of seeing classmates was always complicated, challenging and at times profoundly lonely, even without the added torment of being teased and bullied. A couple of years' ago, Tehilla recalls how she hit a new low: She wanted to become a counsellor for her local Bnei Akiva youth group, and everyone was dead set against it.

The local branch of Bnei Akiva didn't want her, the local kids didn't want her, the management didn't want her – all for different reasons, and all citing that they were acting out of what they believed to be pure motives, i.e., the job would be too difficult for Tehilla, given her disability.

After years' of fighting for 'normalcy', self-respect, and to be treated as a real, feeling person by her peers, this latest rejection was almost too much to bear. Tehilla retreated into profound sadness and depression, stopped eating, and spent most of her time in her room crying, while her family looked on helpless, unsure how to try to help her.

Then, Tehilla made a decision: she wasn't going to give up! Tough as it was to keep standing up again, and to keep on trying, that was the path she decided to continue to walk down, with God's help and her family's unwavering support.

She came out of her room and told her parents that she still wanted to be a counsellor for Bnei Akiva, so the family started lobbying on her behalf – just as they'd lobbied years' earlier for her to be able to attend 'normal' school, and on many other occasions down the years. Eventually, Bnei Akiva capitulated, and Tehilla became a counsellor.

Initially, her group of young charges were less than impressed that they had a 'weird', blind counsellor; but after a few weeks', they softened up and by the end of the year, they'd come to appreciate Tehilla for who she really was, and how much care, attention and effort she put into them, and into planning the group activities.

Now, you might be wondering how it is I know so many of these details about Tehilla. The answer is that last year, Tehilla and her two musically-talented older brothers decided to turn Tehilla's life-story into a kind of musical 'show', that they're now taking all over Israel, particularly to girls' schools.

Tehilla has a hauntingly beautiful voice, and together with her brother Oren, she's written many songs describing her difficulties and her triumphs. She intersperses these songs with the story of what was happening to her at various points in her life, with the aim of driving a few crucially-important points home to her audience, like:

1. Everyone has a choice about how they react to the pain and suffering they experience in their lives. They can either get embittered, give up and go sour, or they can dig deep, hold on to God, and CHOOSE to turn their suffering into something good and life-affirming.

2. No-one should underestimate the power words have to damage other people – or build them up. The girls who teased Tehilla so cruelly had no idea what daggers they were casting into her heart, or how it literally took her years' to recover her self-confidence. By the same token, the words of support and love her family continued to pour into her made all the difference to Tehilla being able to come through her experiences stronger, and wanting to make a difference in the world.

3. Emuna is what gets us through all the heart wrenching difficulties that every single one of us has to face.

When Tehilla came to perform for a group of 11-13 year old girls plus their parents in my daughter's school, there was barely a dry eye in the house.

I'd gone to the evening obsessing over all my (very minor) difficulties with my book, my sense of purpose, my washing (an ongoing challenge...) and I came out so grateful and inspired.

What amazing Jews there are in the world! What a privilege to share an evening like that with someone like Tehilla. Let me leave you with some of her parting words.

"I want the world to be a place where people don't just see the externals, like you do, but where they see the inside of a person, and feel who they really are, like I do," she said. And I realized that for all that she's completely bling, Tehilla actually sees things much clearer than the rest of us.

The good enough mother

God always has a sense of humor: in the middle of me pulling together a huge mountain of evidence that 'science' is increasingly coming to the view that parental emotional neglect is at the heart of pretty much every mental and emotional difficulty you care to mention, from the biggest to the smallest, I suddenly realized that I'm spending far too much time typing, and not enough time interacting with my own family.

There I was, mulling over the whole concept of the 'good enough mother', and related ideas about being a 'good enough Jew', when it struck me that I spent most of yesterday ignoring all my family so I could get another few thousand words of my next book typed up.

One kid had just spent two whole days doing a bunch of amazing volunteer mitzvah activities with Bnei Akiva – and I was too tired to ask her anything about it. Another was clearly bored, but I gave her some cash to buy a 'NeoCube' and then went back to my computer, relieved to have got out of having to do anything more 'hands on' and interactive.

And my husband? What, that guy that takes out the rubbish and sings zemirot on Shabbat? Well, he got back from Uman a couple of days' ago, and I've still only heard a fraction of his crazy stories.

Hmmm.

Not unusually in my life, things had got out of balance again.

When my kids were small, and I had a career (that actually paid me really good money...) I realized I had to choose between putting my family first, or working, because I couldn't do both. When I quit work, it was the best decision I ever made – and also the hardest. Writing is in my blood. Interacting and communicating is my life-force. But I just knew that if I didn't take a few years' off from pursuing 'my interests' my kids were going to end up emotional and spiritual wrecks.

The last few years, I've had to fix so many things in myself, and I came to a point last year where I thought I'd learnt enough lessons about what was *really* important to risk pursuing 'my interests' again. And generally speaking, I think that's probably true. But I'm learning that every day is still a challenge, and every day I have to take the time to ask the questions all over again:

>> Am I being a 'good enough' mother?
>> Am I being a 'good enough' wife?
>> Am I being a 'good enough' friend?
>> Am I being a 'good enough' Jew?

And recently, the answer has been coming back a bit too often: "no, you're not! You're getting too preoccupied with minutiae again, you're losing track of the importance of people, of the beauty of a walk or conversation with someone you care for that isn't 'goal-orientated'."

I bet you'd like to know how I'm defining 'good enough'...

Well, it's like this: Good enough is definitely NOT full-time perfect, 100% altruistic and angelic. If it was, no-one could achieve it, which would kind of defeat the whole point.

'Good enough' is a state where generally, I put my kids and husband and God and my own soul first *enough of the time* to let them know I care about them, I love them, and that they are the most important things in the world to me.

That doesn't mean that I immediately stop what I'm doing every time my kid or husband wants something, for example, but that I stop *enough times* for them to know that if I didn't stop on this occasion, either what I'm doing is really important, or what they want is really not.

Being 'good enough' means that when I know I'm dropping the ball, I don't just sweep that understanding under the carpet or make excuses; I try to fix the problem. So today, once I realized that it wasn't 'good enough' that I hadn't taken the time to ask my kid about her volunteering experiences, I decided to walk her to the bus-stop this morning, so she could share with me, a little.

I was so pleased I did that. I felt like the balance was starting to swing back again towards 'good enough' again, just in time.

Being a parent, being a mother, is a huge responsibility, especially in this generation of emotional disconnect. If I wasn't regularly taking time-outs to try and evaluate my life and behavior, I shudder to think how bad things could get before I'd take my head out of the computer and realize that my family, my children, my marriage were melting down.

And I don't have Wi-Fi at home...And I don't have an i-Phone... And I barely spend any time at all doing 'extra-curricular' activities with girlfriends, or having hour long catch up sessions on the phone.

And I'm still struggling to be 'good enough'.

I know this isn't easy reading. But I want you to know, dear wife, dear mother, that you, me and all of us CAN achieve that level of 'good enough' where our kids will turn out emotionally and spiritually-healthy, and know that they're loved.

And here's a few things that will help us along the way:

1. Brutal honesty. Often, we're not 'good enough'. Often, the internet, the TV, Facebook, and all the other external 'fluff', materialism and superficiality our lives are crammed with are taking up too much space in our lives

2. Huge amounts of self-compassion. It makes all the difference in the world that we want to be better, and that we want to be 'good enough'. All of us really do love our kids tremendously, and it's so important to acknowledge that, and that we at least WANT to be 'good enough' for them (even if we're not....)

3. Massive amounts of humility. Without God in the picture, and regular introspection, we're not going to come anywhere near to really being 'good enough'

4. Optimism and hope. Even when we've messed it up, and wrecked the relationship, and acted consistently selfishly, it often only takes one sincere gesture, one genuine apology, one attempt to validate and accept the other person's hurt feelings, to tip the whole thing back over into the measure of 'good enough' again.

Alone

In recent years, every time we get to parsha Mikeitz, where Yosef HaTzaddik is finally freed from prison, and finally gets to see what all his suffering, loneliness and pain was *for*, I find myself getting in a funny mood.

You're meant to find yourself in every letter of the Torah. Somehow, God's put a coded message for every single one of us into every nuance, detail and cantillation mark. Sometimes, you need to be a genius like Rebbe Nachman or the Vilna Gaon to be able to work them out. Other times, the messages hit you so forcefully, it's impossible to miss them.

Yesterday, I was reading the Parsha Mikeitz, and it was when I got to the bit when Yosef starts sobbing when he sees his brothers that it struck me: the man went through a personal *Shoah*. He'd lost his home, his family, everything he held dear, his freedom and his status. He almost lost his soul, when enticed by Potiphar's wife, and then he probably lost his faith in humanity (again...) when he was unfairly incarcerated as a result of doing the right thing.

How was it that he didn't lose his faith in God, after being stuck in a hellish Egyptian prison for 12 years, all alone? The fact that he didn't shows how much of a Tzaddik he truly was. But existential loneliness, when God hides His face from you, and you have no-one in your life to love, or to love you back, is one of the worst punishments known to man.

Somehow, Yosef came through all that. He finally got out of prison. He finally rebuilt his life, albeit still all alone in his Egyptian splendor, with no old friends to reminisce with, no siblings to joke around with, or remember things with, and no parents to encourage him from the side, and tell him how proud they are of him.

And then his brothers show up, and Yosef has to set a chain of events in train that will atone for their previous misdeeds against him, and rectify them for the future. And in the middle of all this, Yosef suddenly realizes that *these are his brothers.* He's reunited with his family physically, but spiritually and mentally, he suddenly realizes that what was, was. It can't be regained, it can't be rebuilt on the same foundations, because such a huge shift has occurred to the very foundation of who Yosef now is.

He's a man who was sold out by his family, and treated mercilessly by the people who should have loved him the most. He's a man who had to face the most difficult alien exile alone, bereft of all sources of comfort except his faith that God would eventually remember him, and turn it all around. He's a man for who all the illusions and pretensions people like to have that 'they are there for each other', and that 'they really care about each other', and that 'you don't have to suffer alone' had disappeared like smoke. And once those daydreams go, you can't get them back for all the wishing in the world.

So I think he was crying a little about how things used to be, and what had been lost, and what had been done to him. But mostly, he was crying because even though they were all reunited again, really, he was as alone as ever. Maybe even more so.

The brothers could never go back to being true 'brothers' to Yosef, because even though he forgave them unconditionally, they couldn't forgive themselves. Yosef was a permanent, and permanently uncomfortable, reminder to them of their own flaws and limitations and capacity for evil, and there was nothing Yosef could do to erase that knowledge, and truly regain his family.

I think this story has to resonate for anyone who's a baal teshuva; anyone who's made Aliya; anyone who found their life going in a direction that changed them fundamentally, even for best of reasons. The ultimate outcome is only good, the spiritual rewards are more than worth the pain and the effort.

But the aloneness of it all seems to stay with you forever.

Welcome back, green jumper

A couple of days' back, one of my kids came to me with a strange complaint: she was having troubles remembering stuff. She couldn't remember what our last house looked like, what she'd just learned for an exam etc. etc.

First things first: I freaked out, and started imagining all the worst possible scenarios, God forbid. Then, God calmed me down a bit and I realized that my kid is completely sleep-deprived, and operating in zombie mode. We had a chat about doing less social activities, and trying to get at least 6-7 hours' sleep a night, regularly, and I felt a bit happier and calmer.

But still not 100%.

So the next day, I had a long chat with God about it all, because He likes to use my kids to bring my attention to things I've been sweeping under the carpet, and I had the feeling that another 'message' had just been delivered, that needed decoding and responding to. Sure enough, I lifted up the corner of that particular mental rug, and all this icky stuff started tumbling out.

To cut a long story short, the last two years' has been about me and my husband trying to find the 'real us' in the middle of all the pseudo-frum, keeping up appearances stuff that can happen in the baal teshuva world (and many other places, too).

For many years, we were taking our cues from people who were far more superficial, and far less 'plugged in' to authentic Yiddishkeit than was apparent. Last year, my main influencer and my husband's main influencer were both revealed as religious phonies within a week of each other – and the impact stuck us harder than anything else we experienced in that terrible two years.

Thank God for my rabbi. He's what kept me and my husband afloat, as we struggled to find ourselves in the wreckage of who we thought we really were, and what we'd been told, and all the confusion about what God *really* wanted from us, given that we'd been following advice for years that had come from a very warped source – and our lives were in tatters, as a direct result.

When my influencer got unmasked as a religious phony I found it so hard to deal with that I kind of shut down for a year. I dealt with whatever I had to, to keep functioning and keep my faith going at even a basic level (and even that was hard enough, let me tell you.) But I couldn't even begin to face a lot of the bigger questions that the whole situation had dragged up, so I swept them under the carpet.

And so did my husband.

We forgot. At least, we tried to. We tried to blank all the feelings of anger, denial about what had happened, betrayal, hatred, vengeance etc., and carry on being good, sweet Jews.

But God showed me with my daughter's 'memory blanks' that it was time to lift the lid on the whole sordid mess, and begin to deal with the rest of the fall-out. So yesterday, I began that process, and it's already been very helpful.

Already, I'm starting to get clearer and clearer that the people who encourage others to rush out and 'dress the part' regardless of what's going on internally are coming from a warped, superficial place.

People who lack compassion for the human struggle and effort that is involved in keeping even the most basic mitzvahs in today's world, are coming from a warped, superficial place.

People who love acting like 'Rabbi Rockstars', where the emphasis is all about their personalities, and their 'amazing' spiritual level, and their 'amazing' Torah shiurim on YouTube and their 'amazing' Twitter posts – are coming from a warped, superficial place.

If 'Rabbi Rockstar' can't tell you how he sometimes struggles to get out of bed in the morning; or if he casually gossips about other Torah figures; or, if he likes to suggest, directly or otherwise, this his prayers caused barren women to give birth, or cured cancer, or held off World War III for another 20 years, or any other of that self-serving clap-trap that is unfortunately so commonplace, and so believed by the gullible masses – get the heck away.

Real rabbis are just that: real. They understand your pain, they share your problems, and they give you practical advice how to pull through.

By contrast, one of our phony influencers told us the reason we were having such a hard time last year was because my husband hadn't shaved all his hair off, the authentic Breslev way, when he decided to grow his payot. The man told us this with such contempt in his voice, and such disdain for us in his eyes, that it broke the spell I'd been under for years.

All the effort to improve, all the huge self-sacrifice we'd made to try to give God what we thought He wanted, at enormous cost to us in just about every way – and this phony had the audacity to suggest that all God really cared about was that my husband hadn't shaved his head!

It was so ludicrous I almost laughed out loud! But at that point it showed me so clearly that external appearances were really all that counted for our religious phony, and that he'd been advising us from that pretend, intolerant, judgmental, superior and superficially-pious place for years, without us realizing what was going on.

For weeks, even months, afterwards, I was so angry about it all. I couldn't trust myself to write or talk about what had happened. But now it's time to remember it again, and to look those questions about what really God does and does not want from us, square in the face.

God wants the heart

For years, I'd been blindly following people who externally look the part, but who were really very far away from compassion, truth, and emuna, as they led me down a path of increasing religious severity and external piety. The whole time, I was thinking that God really wanted me to graduate to a place of padded head-bands and bullet-proof stockings, and that *that* would be the pinnacle of kedusha and Yiddishkeit in my life.

Man, I was so miserable being religious like that! I felt like I'd lost everything that made me 'me', from my favorite jeans skirt, to my permission to read secular books, to my ability to reach out and relate to people who weren't super-machmir-frum-angels.

Then God did my the biggest favor of my life (although it didn't feel like that at the time): He showed me that the people who were running off their mouths the loudest about other people's flaws; and who were putting on the biggest show of being unimpeachable, super-holy rollers; and who were full of criticism of others and competition and superiority about their own apparently lofty religious levels - were actually very flawed people, with hugely problematic character traits.

They were selfish, jealous, competitive, untruthful, insecure and arrogant.

But they'd had me fooled for years, because they dressed impeccably in black and white, had big shtreimels, and 'ticked all the boxes' externally, 100%. But they were living a huge lie, and the main people they were lying to about what was really going on was themselves.

I had such a strong reaction against these religious hypocrites last year that it's only because God and my rabbi were hanging on to me so tightly that I didn't walk away from an observant lifestyle.

It's taken me months of praying and searching and asking God for help to really emerge out of the other side of the experience, but I think that's the stage I'm now at. I want to tell you what I went through, and what I learnt from it all, so it can hopefully help you to avoid having to go through the same sort of heartache and confusion.

There is so much that could be said, but I'm going to concentrate on two things, to try to make my point: the latest Star Wars movie, and my husband's green jumper.

Last week, I saw an ad for another Star Wars installment, replete with an ancient-looking Harrison Ford (is that a wig, or what?) and all the latest hi-tech hoopla. I got pretty weird after I saw the ad, and started to feel all weepy, but didn't know why.

After some introspection it struck me that I've seen every one of the previous six Star Wars movies, and they were kind of 'movie milestones' that cemented other key things in place that were going on in my life. In short, Star Wars isn't just a movie for me, it's a kind of self-reference point, a way of me pegging myself in the world. And now, that frame of reference was gone, and I was feeling pretty lost again about who I really was.

Then, the little voice in my head told me: "give yourself permission to go and see it." So I did: I imagined getting it out on DVD; sitting down at my pc to watch it, how it would look, how I would feel before, during and afterwards. And at the end of that process, I knew with complete certainty: I *do not* want to watch this! It's a waste of time, and will fill my head and soul with a lot of damaging stuff.

I felt so good! The old 'superficially-religious' me would never have heard that little voice out because I'd have been far too worried about 'where is this going to lead...' – which means that really, I'd have been really pining to see the movie on the inside, where stuff really counts. This way, I brought the whole issue out into the open, and I CHOSE not to see the movie. And the difference is enormous.

Next, I came and had a serious talk with my husband about the whole 'package' we got sold by the religious phonies a few years' back, who made us feel like we were so materialistic for doing things like holding down a job, wanting a nice place to live, and not devoting ourselves to the cause (i.e., their cause...) 24/7.

Thanks to them, my husband felt like he was a terrible person for working. Thanks to them, we both felt like we were letting God down, every time we wanted to take a day's holiday, or buy something new that wasn't directly connected to keeping shabbat or a Yom Tov. Thanks to them, we ended up financially broke, spiritually broken and completely alone in the world, trying to jump through more and more impossible hoops to keep their harsh version of God appeased.

(Yes, I know it was all from God, and all for the good, but that's an idea for another time.)

So I came and asked my husband: that favorite olive green jumper of yours, which you couldn't quite throw away, even though it wasn't black or white. Do you think God would mind if you wore it again? Do you think you'll be letting God down, somehow, if you decided that the 'real you' likes wearing olive green jumpers?

He looked at me shocked. But now he's thinking it over, and we'll see what happens next.

The point is not that he should, or shouldn't wear it: the point is, that he, and me, and all of us, should be asking ourselves *what does God really want?*

Because there's a lot of people out there telling us that God wants padded head-bands, and impossible religious perfection, and miserable, super-machmir, intolerant, superficial

Yiddishkeit that looks so impressive, but feels so horribly wrong.

But really? God wants the heart. And if it happens to come packaged in an olive green jumper, I have a feeling that's fine by Him.

About the author

///

Rivka Levy has been writing professionally for more than 20 years (*gosh, that makes me sound really old...*) and is the author of eight books on God-based holistic health and Jewish thought (*but at least that bit made me sound really clever...*).

Rivka lives (*in a rented shoebox*) in Jerusalem with her husband and two daughters (*but the huge mansion is on its way, bezrat Hashem.*)

You can read more of Rivka's not-so-secret diary at her popular blog for Jewish women, www.emunaroma.com.

Coming Soon!

**The Secret Diary of a Jewish Housewife
VOLUME II**

CPSIA information can be obtained
at www.ICGtesting.com
Printed in the USA
LVOW03s1436280817
546678LV00001B/235/P